RIKSANTIKVARIEÄMBETET ARKEOLOGISKA UNDERSÖKNINGAR SKRIFTER 45

Urban Diversity
Archaeology in the Swedish Province of Östergötland

Urban Diversity

Archaeology in the Swedish Province of Östergötland

Edited by Rikard Hedvall

Hans Andersson
Lars Ersgård
Rikard Hedvall
Pär Karlsson
Karin Lindeblad
Lena Lindgren-Hertz
Hanna Menander
Ann-Lili Nielsen
Göran Tagesson

The National Heritage Board

Riksantikvarieämbetets förlag

Box 5405, SE-114 84 Stockholm, Sweden

Phone +46 (0)8-519 180 00

Fax +46 (0)8-519 180 83

E-mail bocker@raa.se

www.raa.se

Cover picture The inner city of Norrköping. Photo: Jan Norrman (RAÄ)

Production and layout Britt Lundberg (RAÄ)

Translation Alan Crozier

Photography Håkan Ahldén, Göran Billeson, Lars Ekelund, Rikard Hedvall (RAÄ),
Jens Heimdahl, Karin Lindeblad (RAÄ), Pål-Nils Nilsson, Jan Norrman (RAÄ), National Archives

Graphics Lars Östlin (RAÄ)

National Land Survey maps © Lantmäteriverket, S-801 82 Gävle, Sweden. Dnr L 1999/3

Printed by Tryckhuset, Linköping 2002

Riksantikvarieämbetet Arkeologiska undersökningar Skrifter 45
1:1
ISSN 1102-187X
ISBN 91-7209-265-3

Contents

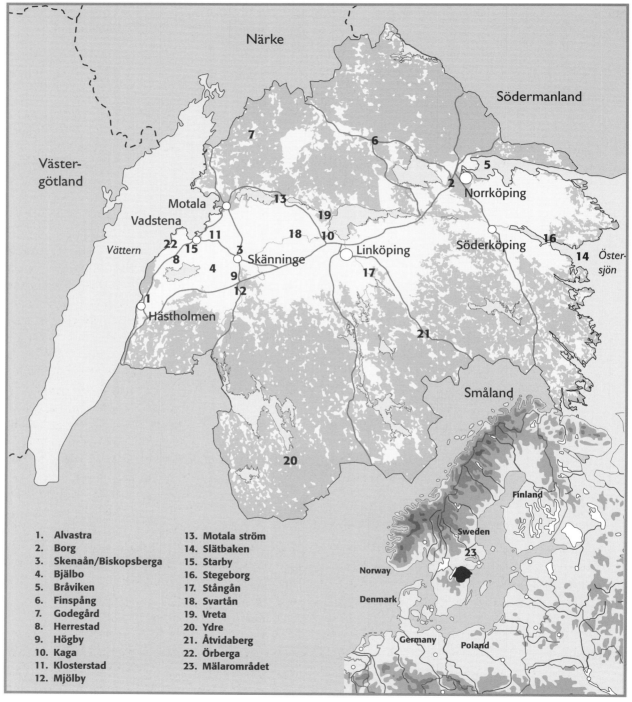

1.	Alvastra	13.	Motala ström
2.	Borg	14.	Slätbaken
3.	Skenaån/Biskopsberga	15.	Starby
4.	Bjälbo	16.	Stegeborg
5.	Bråviken	17.	Stångån
6.	Finspång	18.	Svartån
7.	Godegård	19.	Vreta
8.	Herrestad	20.	Ydre
9.	Högby	21.	Åtvidaberg
10.	Kaga	22.	Örberga
11.	Klosterstad	23.	Mälarområdet
12.	Mjölby		

Map of Northern Europe and Östergötland, showing the names of the places, lakes, and watercourses mentioned in the articles. Graphics: Lars Östlin, RAÄ.

Urban Archaeology in Östergötland

Swedish urban archaeology underwent a huge upswing in the 1970s and 1980s. In the spirit of the time, older buildings in towns and cities were to be replaced with modern business complexes and multi-storey car parks. It could not be taken for granted then that medieval deposits would be investigated before new buildings were constructed. It later became the normal practice for urban occupation layers to be protected by law, which means that anyone who wishes to build and remove occupation layers must pay the cost of an archaeological investigation. From having formerly been a research field for historians, urban studies became an interdisciplinary field. During the 1990s the pressure of development in towns decreased. Large infrastructure investments in roads and railways have led to an increase in the investigation of medieval remains in the countryside. Parallel to these, the National Heritage Board in Östergötland (RAÄ, UV Öst) has carried out major excavations in the medieval towns, on a greater scale than in any other Swedish province. In the last few years, remains from the modern period, after the 1550s, have also been investigated in towns.

The aim of this publication is to shed light on current problems in urban archaeology in Östergötland through a number of articles. It does not claim to be a comprehensive picture of the medieval towns in the province. The book begins with this brief survey of the towns in Östergötland. This is followed by a short description of the background to the medieval province. There are then six articles dealing with early medieval and late medieval central places, spatiality in the medieval town, and various methodological approaches in urban archaeology. The book concludes with some more general and theoretical reflections on the process of urbanization in Östergötland and the rest of Sweden.

"The Medieval Town" project

When one discusses Swedish urban archaeology, it is impossible to avoid mentioning the project that has set its stamp on the view of the medieval town at several different levels. As a direct consequence of the increased pressure of development in Swedish towns in the 1970s, a project was started entitled "The Consequences of the Early Urbanization Process for Present-Day Planning", known for short as "The Medieval Town". The project was directed by Hans Andersson, later professor of medieval archaeology, as a collaborative venture between the National Heritage Board and the Department of Medieval Archaeology in Lund. One of the main aims was to provide a foundation for cultural heritage management (Andersson 1978). The project has resulted in more than 70 reports, one for each place that the project defined as a medieval town. These describe all the archaeological interventions, present parts of the written source material, and discuss future problem areas. The project also published reports dealing with more general questions concerning urbanization, including the final report from 1990 (Andersson 1990).

The urbanization of places was discussed and defined on the basis of the following three kinds of criteria: *functional*, *topographical*, and *judicial-administrative* (Andersson 1978, p. 6; Andersson 1990, pp. 26 ff.). These may be said to correspond respectively to the concepts of *central place*, *built-up area*, and *town*. A central place, from this perspective, can be described

as a place fulfilling special functions common to a larger hinterland. The place may have been a centre because, for example, a church, market, specialized craft, or court was located in it. A built-up area refers to permanent settlement of a larger size than settlements in the surrounding agrarian countryside. A central place and built-up area can be described as a town when it also distinguishes itself from the hinterland by having its own judicial system and its own forms of government. This definition is only applicable to high medieval and late medieval towns. An early medieval place is characterized as a town if it was both a central place and a built-up area and/or if it is referred to as a town in contemporary written sources.

The above definition of a medieval town can of course be questioned and discussed, for example, as regards the emphasis on the written sources and the absence of qualitative distinctions between towns (see e.g. Andrén 1985; Carelli 2001, pp. 104 ff.).

The medieval towns

In Östergötland there are six places that can be regarded as medieval towns according to the criteria listed above (Andersson 1990). Urbanization in these places differed greatly as regards time and content. The character and thickness of the medieval deposits also varies greatly, as does the state of our knowledge. Several of the places have little in common apart from the fact that they received borough charters in the Middle Ages.

The towns are all in the central plain of Östergötland, at fairly equal distances from each other. On the coast are the towns of Norrköping and Söderköping, each in a bay of the Baltic Sea. Skänninge and Linköping are in the fertile plains of the interior. Vadstena and Hästholmen are situated on the large Lake Vättern. This regularity in the distance between the towns

Fig. 1. Söderköping was one of Sweden's most important ports in the Middle Ages. The town has basically retained its extent and its street grid until the present day. Photo: Jan Norrman, RAÄ.

has been interpreted as indicating control by a central power (Andersson 1990, p. 83).

In Östergötland there are no parallels to the early medieval towns of Sigtuna, Visby, and Lund, which can be characterized as towns as early as the end of the tenth century or the start of the eleventh century. The places in Östergötland do not emerge as towns until the thirteenth century. On the other hand, Norrköping, Söderköping, Linköping, and Skänninge have been held up as early medieval central places. They all show an early ecclesiastical centrality, with two early churches, a feature that they share with several contemporary central Swedish central places. In Söderköping and Skänninge there are also archaeological remains with traces of early crafts which can be associated with this early period (Hasselmo 1992). In the course of the Middle Ages these places became towns, although the process of urbanization took very different forms. Vadstena and Hästholmen are both late medieval town formations, each intimately associated with its monastic institution (Andersson 1990, pp. 46 ff.). Below is a very brief presentation of what is known about the individual towns.

Gateway to the Baltic
Söderköping is at the point in the province where the rivers Storån and Lillån meet and then flow into the Baltic Sea. Via the waterways the town had good communications with the interior. Söderköping is the town in Östergötland with the longest archaeological tradition and also the town that is best illuminated by excavations. The medieval deposits are thick, containing very well-preserved remains, and archaeologists regard it as a type example of what a medieval town ought to look like. The town has long played an important part in urban studies. As early as the 1920s, the art historian Erik Lundberg carried out investigations in Söderköping and published hypotheses about the medieval topography of the town (Lundberg 1928).

In Söderköping a series of large-scale investigations were conducted from the 1970s to the start of the 1990s, when the most recent major excavation was carried out in the town centre. Söderköping may be defined as an early medieval central place, with two early churches, one on either side of the river. The location of the place in the landscape is characteristic of an early medieval central place: beside a watercourse broken by waterfalls, a natural reloading place. The results of the investigations show that there was early medieval settlement within a relatively large area, above all beside the Storån, where land and water routes crossed. Remains of the early central place have been interpreted as an initially non-permanent settlement which later acquired a more lasting character with craft activities. The archaeological findings show that the thirteenth-century town emerged during the first decades of the century. By the mid-thirteenth century the place seems already to have reached its full extent, when it covered an area of about 900 by 400 metres (Tesch 1987; Hasselmo 1992).

The place is described in early written sources as a town. A Franciscan friary was established here as early as 1235. Mendicant orders mainly built their houses in towns, so there is good reason to assume that Söderköping at this time was regarded as a town. A burgher of Söderköping is mentioned in the mid-thirteenth century, and in the 1280s there was a mint here (Broberg and Hasselmo 1978). At the end of the Middle Ages Söderköping declined in importance, giving way to the neighbouring town of Norrköping.

The town in the centre of the countryside
Skänninge is located by the River Skenaån, centrally placed in a prehistoric agricultural district. There are a large number of runestones and early Romanesque burial monuments in and around the town, known as Eskilstuna cists. On each side of the river there was an early Romanesque church. Like Söderköping, the place became urbanized early on. In 1237 the Dominicans set up a friary here, burghers are mentioned in the mid-thirteenth century, and in 1287 there is a record of a mint. Around 1300 yet another church was built in the town (Hasselmo 1983). Skänninge likewise attracted scholarly attention early on. In 1921 Sven T.

Kjellberg presented a reconstruction of the town's medieval topography. It was viewed as a typical example of how a thirteenth-century town grew up around an earlier market place. There has not been as much archaeological study as in Söderköping, and no major excavations have been conducted since the end of the 1970s. Smaller investigations at a few places in the town, after the report for "The Medieval Town" was written, have uncovered remains that are older than the establishment of the town proper in the thirteenth century (Hasselmo 1987).

The small town by the big fisheries

Norrköping lies where the River Motala flows into the Baltic Sea. There are a large number of falls in the river which were used at an early stage for mills and permanent fisheries. In the Early Middle Ages it can be described as a central place with two early churches. It was urbanized in the mid-fourteenth century, but it was a weak town formation with few institutions. In the early modern period the town underwent an enormous expansion, when it started its development into one of Sweden's biggest industrial cities (Broberg 1984). UV Öst did extensive archaeological work in Norrköping during the 1990s. Medieval Norrköping had previously been very difficult to capture archaeologically. Thanks to the recent excavations, however, archaeologists are beginning to put together a picture of a settlement localized on the bank of the River Motala and not, as previously assumed, in the area around the two medieval churches. Early modern remains in the town have been investigated, and Norrköping is actually the only town in Östergötland where UV Öst has done modern archaeology on any scale.

In the 1990, two large-scale excavations of medieval rural settlement were conducted on the edge of Norrköping. At the medieval church in Borg, archaeologists investigated a magnate's farm from the Late Iron Age and Middle Ages which is called a royal manor in a fourteenth-century source (Lindeblad 1996; Nielsen 1996). On the basis of the excavations in Borg, the urbanization of Norrköping has been discussed in relation to the surrounding Viking Age and medieval landscape. The seemingly weak medieval urbanization is put in a slightly larger spatial context. By studying a larger geographical area around the town, one can obtain a greater understanding both of urbanization in the town and of the surrounding agrarian landscape (Lindeblad 1997).

The bishop's town

Linköping is on the River Stångån, close to where it flows into Lake Roxen. Around the town there is rich agricultural land with settlement going back to prehistoric time. It was an ecclesiastical central place as early as the start of the twelfth century, with two early churches. There is no archaeological material from this time. By the 1120s at the latest, the bishop's seat was located here, but it is not until the end of the thirteenth century that the place begins to stand out as urbanized, with a Franciscan friary among other features. The results of several excavations have shown that it was not until the fourteenth century that Linköping began to be established as a built-up area.

The pre-industrial landscape around Linköping has been treated in the publication *Kring Stång*. This discusses, among other things, the relation between the surrounding countryside and the town (Borna Ahlkvist and Tollin 1994). There have been several major excavations on the edge of Linköping in recent years. These have above all concerned habitation sites from the Early Iron Age, but a few investigations, all undertaken at the sites of later villages, have shown that settlement was established there by the Late Iron Age, with site continuity until the present day (Lindgren Hertz 1997).

The convent town

Vadstena has long been of interest to historians, chiefly concerned with the convent and Saint Birgitta. Vadstena distinguishes itself from the towns of Östergötland by being a late medieval foundation. The emergence of the town was intimately associated with the establishment of the Birgittine convent at the end of the fourteenth century. In the Late Middle Ages Vadstena was a cultural and spiritual centre, and the many well-preserved late medieval stone buildings still give the town a special character. Before the actual town was established there was a palace of the Folkunga dynasty from the thirteenth century. Close to the palace was a Romanesque church, and we know from written sources that there was also a village; it has not been located by archaeologists.

Around Vadstena there are a large number of well-preserved early Romanesque churches. In the project "The Churches in Dal Hundred", run by the National Heritage Board's division for the churches of Sweden, several of these have been analysed in recent years (Bonnier 1996). In Klosterstad, a few kilometres out-

side Vadstena, an ongoing project concerns a newly discovered round church. The project is run by staff from UV Öst in collaboration with the National Heritage Board's divisions working with churches, runic inscriptions, and medieval Sweden. A survey of the project has been published in the journal *Fornvännen* (Hedvall and Gustafsson 2001).

The Cistercians' harbour

Turning to the sixth place mentioned as a town in Östergötland, we find ourselves at Hästholmen, at an excellent site for a harbour on the shore of Lake Vättern. Around 1300 this is recorded as an urban setting, *villa forensis*, in a written source. It has been suggested that the emergence of the medieval place

Fig. 2. Öjebro is on the main road that linked Skänninge and Linköping in the Middle Ages. The energy from the waterfalls in the River Svartån was used from the Middle Ages until the nineteenth century to power mills. In the nineteenth century there were still about forty men employed to grind the grain from the fertile plain. Photo: Jan Norrman, RAÄ.

was intimately associated with the nearby Cistercian abbey of Alvastra (Klackenberg 1984). By 1400 the evidence for the urban character of the place already begins to recede. Hästholmen has not been the subject of any archaeological investigations which could shed light on the medieval place.

Around Alvastra an interdisciplinary project is in progress, studying the abbey in a larger context, considering economic and social organization before and after the foundation of the abbey. The relation of the area to the early royal power and the medieval process of town formation will also be discussed by the project. Some of the results of the excavations have already been published (Ersgård 1996; Holmström 1999).

... and those which did not become towns

In archaeological research into urbanization the focus hitherto has mainly been on the places that became towns in a formal sense during the Middle Ages. In the 1980s archaeologists directed their attention to early medieval remains found in several towns. What these older central places have in common is that they emerged as towns in the High and Late Middle Ages (Hasselmo 1992).

A largely unresearched field is the places that show indications of being central places and built-up areas in the Middle Ages but which are not recorded as towns in the extant written sources. In Östergötland, Motala is known to have been a medieval central place and built-up area (see more below). The place is mentioned for the first time in writing in 1288. Throughout the Middle Ages there were a large number of mills and permanent fisheries here, owned by ecclesiastical institutions and the aristocracy. Built-up settlement was established around these, divided into plots occupied by specialist craftsmen. As far as we know, Motala did not receive a borough charter in the Middle Ages, but it rightly belongs in a discussion of urbanization. There is almost certainly a wide range of unresearched central places in Östergötland, contemporary with the towns. As examples of places that may be worth further study, we may mention two other mill sites in western Östergötland: Mjölby and Öjebro. Mills were located by waterfalls, often by large bridges, and they naturally became reloading places which attracted people. In the course of the Middle Ages, mining sites developed in both the southern and the northern forested districts of Östergötland. There are no medieval towns in these mining areas, but Åtvidaberg and Godegård, which enjoyed special privileges, may be interesting to elucidate from the perspective of central places.

Summing up

With this brief survey as a background, we may note that the process of town formation in Östergötland was in no way a uniform phenomenon as regards either the course of urbanization, the state of our knowledge, or the archaeological potential. The state of our knowledge is of course dependent on how much archaeological work has been done, but also on the character of the remains. Norrköping is so difficult to grasp archaeologically that it is essential to shed light on really basic issues. From Söderköping, on the other hand, we have such a large amount of archaeological material that we can now deepen the analysis of urbanization, social topography, and so on a few steps further.

In the Early Middle Ages Söderköping and Skänninge stand out as central places in the archaeological material, each with two early churches. The early medieval deposits are above all concentrated along the rivers flowing through the two places. Söderköping and Skänninge are also the places that stand out most clearly in the written sources as towns, as early as the first half of the thirteenth century. In the 1230s mendicant orders established friaries in both places, and this was where the first hospitals in Östergötland were founded. At the end of the thirteenth century there was a mint in each town, an institution not found in the other towns in Östergötland. Söderköping and Skänninge could possibly be characterized, not just as the earliest urbanized places in the province but also as the *most* urbanized. In the fourteenth century

Norrköping, Vadstena, Linköping, and Hästholmen emerged as urbanized places. Behind the foundation of Vadstena, and perhaps also Hästholmen, were two different monastic orders, the Birgittines in Vadstena and the Cistercians in Alvastra. Norrköping has likewise been described as "a monastic annex" to the Cistercian abbey in Askeby, but this admittedly interesting suggestion has not been further discussed in modern research (Nordén 1917, p. 50). The emergence of Linköping can with great probability be associated with the fact that the place became an episcopal see at an early stage.

On the outskirts of several of the medieval towns, UV Öst has investigated medieval remains in the countryside. The results of these in relation to the towns have only been discussed as regards Norrköping. In the Middle Ages there were a number of places which cannot be defined as either towns or villages. The places can be centres in medieval mining areas or virtually pre-industrial sites with, for example, milling as the main trade. The medieval central places have not attracted much attention in the discussion of urbanization in Östergötland, but they should have a given place in the future. Finally, it may be said that the investigations in the next few years will mean that the study of urbanization can be further illuminated and nuanced. Planned excavations in Skänninge, and Motala will give us a very good opportunity to deepen our knowledge of the interesting and complex urbanization in the province.

■ **Karin Lindeblad**

References

Andersson, H. 1978. *Urbaniseringsprocessen i det medeltida Sverige*. Riksantikvarieämbetets och Statens historiska museer rapport: Medeltidsstaden 7. Stockholm.

Andersson, H. 1990. *Sjuttiosex medeltidsstäder – aspekter på stadsarkeologi och medeltida urbaniseringsprocess i Sverige och Finland*. Riksantikvarieämbetets och Statens historiska museer rapport: Medeltidsstaden 76. Stockholm.

Andrén, A. 1985. *Den urbana scenen. Städer och samhälle i det medeltida Danmark*. Acta Archaeologica Lundensia 13. Lund.

Bonnier, A.-C. 1996. Kyrkorna i Dals härad. Några av landets äldsta kyrkor. *Kyrka i bruk. Meddelanden från Östergötlands Länsmuseum* 1996. Linköping.

Borna Ahlkvist, H., and Tollin, C. 1994. *Kring Stång. En kulturgeografisk utvärdering byggd på äldre lantmäteriakter och historiska kartöverlägg*. RAÄ, Arkeologiska undersökningar, Skrifter 7. Stockholm.

Broberg, B., and Hasselmo, M. 1978. *Söderköping*. Riksantikvarieämbetets och Statens historiska museer rapport: Medeltidsstaden 5. Stockholm.

Broberg, B. 1984. *Norrköping*. Riksantikvarieämbetets och Statens historiska museer rapport: Medeltidsstaden 50. Stockholm.

Carelli, P. 2001. *En kapitalistisk anda. Kulturella förändringar i 1100-talets Danmark*. Lund Studies in Medieval Archaeology 26. Lund.

Ersgård, L. 1996. Religionsskiftet som social förändring. In Kaliff, A., and Engdahl, K. (eds.), *Religion från stenålder till medeltid*. RAÄ, Arkeologiska undersökningar, Skrifter 19. Linköping.

Hasselmo, M. 1982. *Vadstena*. Riksantikvarieämbetets och Statens historiska museer rapport: Medeltidsstaden 36. Stockholm.

Hasselmo, M. 1983. *Skänninge*. Riksantikvarieämbetets och Statens historiska museer rapport: Medeltidsstaden 40. Stockholm.

Hasselmo, M. 1987. Skänninge. In Andrae, T., Hasselmo, M., and Lamm. K. (eds.), *7000 år på 20 år. Arkeologiska undersökningar i Mellansverige.* RAÄ. Stockholm.

Hasselmo, M. 1987. Sammanfattning. In Andrae, T., Hasselmo, M., and Lamm. K. (eds.), *7000 år på 20 år. Arkeologiska undersökningar i Mellansverige.* RAÄ. Stockholm.

Hasselmo, M. 1992. From Early-Medieval Central-Places to High-Medieval Towns – Urbanization in Sweden from the End of the 10th Century to c. 1200. In Ersgård, L., Holmström, M., and Lamm, K. (eds.), *Rescue and Research. Reflections of Society in Sweden 700 – 1700 A.D.* RAÄ, Arkeologiska undersökningar, Skrifter 2. Stockholm.

Hedvall, R., and Gustafsson, H. 2001. Rundkyrkan i Klosterstad – en presentation av ett pågående projekt. *Fornvännen* 96.

Holmström, M. 1999. Alvastra i statsbildningstid. In Andersson, K., Lagerlöf, A., and Åkerlund, A. (eds.), *Forskaren i fält – en vänbok till Kristina Lamm.* RAÄ, Avdelningen för Arkeologiska undersökningar, Skrifter 27. Stockholm.

Klackenberg, H. 1984. *Hästholmen.* Riksantikvarieämbetets och Statens historiska museer rapport: Medeltidsstaden 59. Stockholm.

Lindeblad, K. 1996. Borgs socken – förändringar i tid och rum 200 – 1200 e Kr. In Lundqvist, L., Lindeblad, K., Nielsen, A.-L., and Ersgård, L. (eds.), *Slöinge och Borg. Stormansgårdar i öst och väst.* RAÄ, Arkeologiska undersökningar, Skrifter 18. Linköping.

Lindeblad, K. 1997. The Town and the Three Farms. On the Organization of the Landscape in and around a Medieval Town. In Andersson, H., Carelli, P., and Ersgård, L. (eds.), *Visions of the Past. Trends and Traditions in Swedish Medieval Archaeology.* Lund Studies in Medieval Archaeology 19. RAÄ, Arkeologiska undersökningar, Skrifter 24. Stockholm.

Lindgren-Hertz, L. 1997. Farm and Landscape. Variations on a Theme in Östergötland. In Andersson, H., Carelli, P., and Ersgård, L. (eds.), *Visions of the Past. Trends and Traditions in Swedish Medieval Archaeology.* Lund Studies in Medieval Archaeo-

logy 19. RAÄ, Arkeologiska undersökningar, Skrifter 24. Stockholm.

Lindgren-Hertz, L. 2001. Speglingar av rumslig organisation. Norrköping i ljuset av mindre arkeologiska undersökningar. In Andrén, A., Ersgård, L., Wienberg, J. (eds.), *Från stad till land. En medeltidsarkeologisk resa tillägnad Hans Andersson.* Lund Studies in Medieval Archaeology 29. Stockholm.

Lundberg, E. 1928. *Topografiska undersökningar i Söderköping.* Kungliga Vitterhets Historie och Antikvitetsakademiens handlingar 39:1. Stockholm.

Nielsen, A.-L. 1996. Borg – enda centralplatsen i Norrköpingsbygden? In Lundqvist, L., Lindeblad, K., Nielsen, A.-L., and Ersgård, L. (eds.), *Slöinge och Borg. Stormansgårdar i öst och väst.* RAÄ, Arkeologiska undersökningar, Skrifter 18. Linköping.

Nordén, A. 1917. *Norrköpings medeltid. Ett Diplomatarium Norcopense.* Stockholm.

Tesch, S. 1987. Söderköping. In Andrae, T., Hasselmo, M., and Lamm. K. (eds.), *7000 år på 20 år. Arkeologiska undersökningar i Mellansverige.* RAÄ. Stockholm.

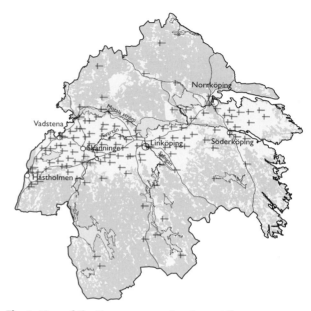

Fig. 1. Map of the Romanesque churches of Östergötland, based on M. Hasselmo, *Skänninge* (Medeltidsstaden 40, Stockholm, 1983). Each church is marked with a cross. The map also shows the medieval towns. Graphics: Lars Östlin, RAÄ.

Introduction

This article is an attempt to describe the cultural history of Östergötland from the eleventh to the sixteenth century from an archaeological perspective. The presentation is in the nature of a survey primarily trying to capture the main tendencies in the historical development. No detailed account of medieval Östergötland has ever been written, despite the rich amount of source material from this era. Much of what is said below is therefore of a hypothetical and preliminary character.

The Early Middle Ages
- Christianization and state formation

The same general spatial pattern that characterized Östergötland in the Iron Age is also found in Early Middle Ages, that is, a concentration of settlement in the fertile plains in the centre of the province, from Lake Vättern in the west to the Baltic Sea in the east. This pattern is evident on a map showing the distribution of Romanesque churches in the province, which moreover displays a clear centre of gravity in western Östergötland, roughly from Vättern to the Linköping area (see Hasselmo 1983, p. 46) (fig. 1). It is difficult to say at present whether this marks a change from the preceding Iron Age situation. The oldest dendrochronological dates hitherto, from the churches of Herrestad and Örberga in western Östergötland, are 1112 and 1116, which suggests that the construction of Romanesque stone churches began in the first decades of the twelfth century (Bonnier 1997, p. 94).

A more crucial watershed between prehistoric and historic times, however, should be sought about a hundred years earlier, around 1000, when several fundamental changes took place in Östergötland. This applies particularly to the process of Christianization. The youngest datings of Late Iron Age cemeteries are from the tenth century (Kaliff 1999, p. 104). The earliest Christian burial places were probably established in the first half of the eleventh century, and some of these were evidently very large. At Alvastra in western Östergötland, one such cemetery has been excavated (Ersgård 1996). It is estimated to have had between 3,000 and 5,000 graves, most of them probably from the eleventh century. In view of the large number of graves and the relatively short period of use, this place must have been a religious centre for a large area, at least bigger than the later parishes. The question how many such early Christian burial places there were, and whether they were all as big as the one in Alvastra, must remain open. The large cemetery could possibly be interpreted as the centre of a new form of cultic community replacing the pagan cult at the magnates' farms of the Late Iron Age. The eleventh-century Christian burial places are likely to be associated with the "Eskilstuna cists", stone burial monuments decorated in the style of runestones, which are more frequent in western Östergötland and which are generally thought to reflect the presence of a social elite (Neill and Lundberg 1994) (fig. 2).

Agrarian settlement seems to have undergone a change in the Viking Age. The archaeological sources for this are not very satisfactory, however, especially as regards the transition from the Late Iron Age to the Early Middle Ages (the eleventh century). Our knowledge of this period is primarily based on a few excavations in the Linköping area. After a thorough-going change during the Migration Period, when Early Iron Age settlement was abandoned, settlement in the Viking Age was established in places which coincide with the later medieval villages. It is still not clear in what form the new settlement units appear during the Viking Age, whether they consisted of one or more farms. A crucial problem is of course when and how the medieval village took shape. The existing source material has partly contradictory indications. Some of the archaeological investigations suggest that settlement was already organized in the Viking Age according to a regulated plan, which agrees in part with the structure of the later villages. Other excavations, however, seem to show that the earliest settlement extended outside the area occupied by the medieval village site, thus suggesting a different organization. The general change in the Viking Age is nevertheless indisputable, which would thus mean a development of agrarian settlement in Östergötland resembling that observed in parts of southern Scandinavia (Lindgren-Hertz 1997, pp. 55 ff.).

In both the Late Iron Age and the Early Middle Ages, Östergötland is generally considered to have been a socially stratified society where a number of powerful families constituted the top social stratum. This elite must have been the main actor behind the early Christian burial places and the later Romanesque churches.

An elite farm environment has been excavated at Borg near Norrköping, and the results shed interesting light on social development in this period (Linde-blad 1996; Nielsen 1996; Lindeblad and Nielsen 1997). After the total restructuring of the landscape at the end of the Migration Period, the farm at Borg was founded in the latter part of the seventh century. A central component of the farm in the Late Iron Age seems to have been a pagan cult house, right beside which hoards of amulet rings and animal bones were found. These categories of find seem to have been deposited outside the cult house. The farm at Borg thus had an obvious religious function in the Late Iron Age, which probably means that it also enjoyed a special social status in the landscape. By all appearances, it belonged to a stratum of "big farms" to which special central functions of a religious-social character were attached.

Fig. 2. Part of the covering slab of a runic burial monument in Viking Age style, known as an Eskilstuna cist, from Klosterstad. The text runs: "... make this tomb after ...". Photo: Göran Billeson.

17

Fig. 3. Bjälbo, the ancestral estate of the Folkunga dynasty. The original stone church was built in the mid-twelfth century. The tower, which was built at the end of the twelfth century, is the only part surviving from the Middle Ages. It is one of the biggest church towers in the province. A wooden church from the eleventh century has been excavated about 100 m north of the stone church, where a small house can be glimpsed between the trees in the picture. Photo: Jan Norrman, RAÄ.

The pagan farm cult at Borg was discontinued in the eleventh century, probably by means of a "ritual burial" of the cult house, but the farm seems to have retained its special social position. There was thus social continuity here from the Late Iron Age into the Middle Ages. It is in early medieval farm settings like Borg that we ought to search for the influential families of magnates that are evident in the written sources from the twelfth century, such as the Stenkil dynasty, the Sverker dynasty, and the Folkunga dynasty. These dominated political life, not just in Östergötland but also on the national level, and they manifested themselves physically in the landscape by building churches and ancestral estates (fig. 3). It is thought that the Stenkil dynasty had Vreta as its main seat, while places like Kaga and Bjälbo has the same status for the Sverker and Folkunga dynasties respectively. The founding of monasteries was also an important part of a social strategy for these families in the twelfth century. It is obvious that the oldest monasteries were established in places which already had a special religious status in the central settlement districts. This is particularly clear in Alvastra, where a Cistercian abbey was founded in 1143. This abbey was placed near the large early Christian burial place established in the eleventh century.

The province of Östergötland is traditionally considered to have played an important role in the process of state formation. It was representatives of the dynasties mentioned above who, alongside members of the rival dynasty of the Erikssons in Västergötland, held the office of king in twelfth- and thirteenth-century Sweden. Against this background, it is interesting to observe the emergence of medieval central places in the landscape, a process that is generally perceived as being closely associated with an active central power. We may begin by noting that Östergötland did not acquire any big early medieval town of the calibre of Lund or Sigtuna. Instead, the central places seem to have a slightly different character.

None of the centrally located towns – Skänninge, Linköping and Norrköping – emerges as a town until the thirteenth century at the earliest, and in Norrköping's case not until the fourteenth century (fig. 1). All three, however, display central functions in an earlier phase. This is mainly expressed through the occurrence of two early churches in each place, which are moreover located on natural communication routes. The centrality thus seems to have an explicit religious character, and in the case of Linköping this is further underlined by the fact that the place became an episcopal see in the first half of the twelfth century. At these early medieval central places there was also secular settlement, although little research has been done on this. Occasional archaeological indications provide hints about the character of this early settlement. In Norrköping an early medieval settlement of limited scale was recently localized beside the River Motala (Motala Ström), possibly adjacent to mills and a fishery (Lindgren-Hertz 2001). In Söderköping in eastern Östergötland, archaeologists have demarcated a larger twelfth-century settlement which had a different structure from the later high medieval town (Broberg and Hasselmo 1978).

The High and Late Middle Ages
- expansion, crisis, and change

The thirteenth century was an expansive century in Östergötland. The most distinct archaeological evidence of this can be found in some of the towns. Generally speaking, however, the medieval urbanization of Östergötland gives a disparate impression, and the development in the individual towns does not seem to follow any uniform pattern.

In Söderköping and Skänninge institutional foundations came as early as the first half of the century. Franciscan friaries were founded in both towns in the 1230s. Söderköping expanded rapidly in the second half of the thirteenth century, reaching its maximum extent at the end of the century. Skänninge may possibly have undergone a similar development (Hasselmo 1983, p. 55). A Franciscan friary was founded in Linköping too, but not until the 1280s. The place must thus have been a fully formed urban centre at the end of the thirteenth century, but we still have no clear archaeological evidence that Linköping expanded to the same extent as Skänninge and Söderköping at this time (Tagesson 1998). Norrköping underwent no expansion during the thirteenth century as regards either institutions or settlement. However, the place probably retained its earlier character of a central place, but with very limited settlement. As the oldest written record suggests, the fishing in the River Motala must have been of vital significance for this settlement (Broberg 1984, p. 13).

To complete the picture of high medieval urbanization in Östergötland one must mention a couple of other places, all of which fall somewhat outside the accepted pattern of medieval urban development. Hästholmen on Lake Vättern is called a *villa forensis* in 1327 and has therefore been defined as an urban formation, the founding of which may have been initiated by the abbey of Alvastra (Klackenberg 1984) (fig. 1). Vadstena is a late medieval town formation which will be considered in more detail below. It became a royal estate in the thirteenth century, however, and the construction of a splendid royal palace around 1260 indicates that Vadstena then must have had special central functions. Motala, located north of Vadstena, is a place which, because of the rich occurrence of mills and fixed fisheries, has been compared to Norrköping, yet Motala never acquired borough status in the Middle Ages; it does seem nevertheless to have had an urban character (Lindeblad 2001).

The Late Middle Ages is generally characterized as a period of profound crisis and social and economic upheaval. As regards the towns of Östergötland, it can also be observed in this connection that the high medieval urban pattern described briefly above was to a certain extent broken.

Norrköping and Vadstena became towns in a formal sense in the Late Middle Ages, with the oldest evidence of urbanization from 1350 and 1382 respectively, but both had been central places before this. The incentive for the town of Vadstena was the Birgittine convent, construction of which began in the 1360s. After the donation of the relics of Saint Birgitta to the convent in the 1370s, Vadstena rapidly grew in importance, and in the fifteenth century it became a major place of pilgrimage and a cultural meeting place. In a spatial sense too, Vadstena grew quickly, starting at the end of the fourteenth century. Nothing comparable happened in Norrköping, which did admittedly undergo some settlement expansion in the Late Middle Ages, but which was still of limited extent at the end of the Middle Ages (Lindgren-Hertz 2001).

As regards the repercussions of the late medieval agrarian crisis on the towns, there is evidence that the construction of the cathedral in Linköping had to be interrupted in the mid-fourteenth century, not to be resumed again until the start of the fifteenth century (Tagesson 1998, p. 114). During this time there seems to have been a change of settlement in this town, whereby the plots were regulated and were more densely built. Urban settlement expanded in the fifteenth century, which also involved the construction of a number of stone houses and stone cellars (ibid.). As for the other towns, both Skänninge and Söderköping seem to have declined in significance after the

fourteenth century. The latter was still an important port at the end of the Middle Ages, however. Little Hästholmen, where we still have no real archaeological traces of urban settlement, lost its urban character in the fifteenth century, with the result that it was just an ordinary village at the start of the sixteenth century.

In the countryside, archaeology has been able to shed much less light on development in the Middle Ages than in the case of the towns. We may nevertheless reckon with a significant expansion of settlement in the thirteenth and fourteenth centuries, colonizing the more peripheral parts of the province north and south of the old central districts (fig. 1). In northern Östergötland it seems that the beginnings of mining were an important incentive to colonization (Nilsson 1990, p. 330).

Not much is known yet about the course of village formation, but written evidence shows that there must have been villages in the Linköping area at the start of the fourteenth century (Borna Ahlkvist and Tollin 1994, p. 33). A characteristic feature of this area, and of the agrarian central districts of Östergötland in general, is that the villages as shown on the earliest maps are mostly quite small in terms of the number of homesteads and that the village sites are usually geometrically regulated. Central questions here are, of course, when this pattern took shape and whether village formation was a protracted process.

A general problem, to which all research on medieval agrarian development must relate, concerns the desertion of settlement that is assumed to have taken place as a consequence of the "late medieval agrarian crisis" in the fourteenth and fifteenth centuries. What was the scale of this desertion, and what long-term consequences did it have for the province of Östergötland? In 1962 the geographer Staffan Helmfrid, in his study of the cultural landscape in Östergötland west of the River Stångån, declared that the late medieval desertion did not have any crucial significance for development here (Helmfrid 1962, p. 86). However, no archaeological investigations have hitherto been able to prove this conclusion. At Ydre in the southern forest district of Östergötland, an interdisciplinary research

Fig. 4. The ruins of Stegeborg castle, strategically located in the bay of Slätbaken, which leads on to the town of Söderköping from the Baltic. The oldest parts of the castle are from the thirteenth century. Photo: Jan Norrman, RAÄ.

project in the 1990s, "Can One Live on a Deserted Farm?", specifically studied the late medieval desertion process. The results have not been published yet, but there is a great deal to suggest that farms were deserted and that this was connected with a reorganization of agrarian production (for more on the project see Widgren 1999).

As regards the churches in the countryside, research hitherto has devoted much more interest to the Early Middle Ages than the Late Middle Ages. Phenomena such as western extensions of the nave, new chancels, and vaulting occur in Östergötland in the later period, but in this the province does not differ much from other areas. In the thirteenth century some churches in western Östergötland were given new cruciform

chancels, an interesting architectural change which seems to have taken place under the influence of Cistercian monastic architecture (Bonnier 1996, p. 84).

The presence of several monastic institutions in the central parts of Östergötland is also thought to have had crucial consequences for social development in the medieval province. Generally speaking, the nobility in Sweden manifested itself with increasing clarity in the Late Middle Ages by creating large estates and building magnificent castles; this appears to have been particularly frequent in the latter part of the fourteenth century. In the rich western Östergötland, however, there are relatively few castles belonging to secular lords, and an explanation suggested for this is that much of the land here was owned by the monasteries

(Lovén 1990, p. 375). A few of the castles in Östergötland have been studied, but this was mostly in early investigations whose basis for dating is not wholly reliable (fig. 4). Most of the castles, however, seem to have been built in the fourteenth century. An example of an unfortified noble estate is Borg near Norrköping, with a tradition going back to the Late Iron Age. This place served as a royal manor throughout the Middle Ages, but in material terms it is only the very rich finds that testify to the social status of the place (Lindeblad and Nielsen 1997).

The start of modern times
- on the way to a new society

The archaeology of the early modern period in Östergötland is still largely undeveloped. I shall conclude by outlining some tendencies in the historical development, on which archaeology should be able to shed light some time in the future.

The sixteenth century was a decisive watershed in Östergötland, as can be observed with particular clarity in urban development. Two important towns in the Middle Ages, Skänninge and Söderköping, then definitively lost their former significance. Linköping and Vadstena likewise underwent a decline in the sixteenth century, due in large part to the Reformation. Vadstena nevertheless retained some of its central role because one of the national castles was built there in the 1540s. In Norrköping, on the other hand, unlike the other towns in Östergötland, a rapid expansion began in the latter part of the sixteenth century. From having been a seemingly insignificant place in the Middle Ages, Norrköping now became the most important town in Östergötland, a position which it was then to retain. Industrial activity on the islets in the river, the export of iron from the mining districts, and extensive sea fishing became the main economic activities of the burghers of Norrköping at the start of the early modern period.

As for the countryside, there was an expansion of settlement in the sixteenth century. A few events in the province may be worth noting as typical of this period. The estate of Borg, which retained its central functions from the Late Iron Age throughout the Middle Ages, was finally closed in the sixteenth century, possibly as a consequence of the rapid expansion of the nearby town of Norrköping. The large monastic property of Alvastra was confiscated by the crown at the Reformation and turned into a royal stock farm. The mining districts of Östergötland underwent a decline in the latter part of the sixteenth century, and mining was increasingly concentrated in one place, Finspång.

These examples suggest that the change in the sixteenth century was of a thoroughgoing structural character and that it affected society in Östergötland on most levels. In certain respects it put an end to lines of development which had been unbroken since the middle of the Iron Age. A new landscape began to take shape, as the economic centre of gravity was increasingly shifted towards the north-eastern part of Östergötland.

■ **Lars Ersgård**

References

Bonnier, A.-C. 1996. Kyrkorna i Dals härad. Några av landets äldsta kyrkor. *Kyrka i bruk. Meddelanden från Östergötlands länsmuseum* 1996.

Bonnier, A.-C. 1997. Det tidiga kyrkobyggandet. In Dahlbäck, G. (ed.), *Kyrka – samhälle – stat. Från kristnande till etablerad kyrka*. Finska Historiska Samfundet. Historiallinen Arkisto 110:3. Helsinki.

Borna Ahlkvist, H., and Tollin, C. 1994. *Kring Stång. En kulturgeografisk utvärdering byggd på äldre lantmäteriakter och historiska kartöverlägg*. RAÄ, Arkeologiska undersökningar, Skrifter 7. Stockholm.

Broberg, B. 1984. *Norrköping*. Riksantikvarieämbetets

och Statens historiska museer rapport: Medeltidsstaden 50. Stockholm.

Broberg, B., and Hasselmo, M. 1978. *Söderköping*.
Riksantikvarieämbetets och Statens historiska museer rapport: Medeltidsstaden 5. Stockholm.

Ersgård, L. 1996. Religionsskiftet som social förändring. Om tidigmedeltida gravskick i Dalarna och
Östergötland. In Engdahl, K., and Kaliff, A. (eds.),
*Religion från stenålder till medeltid. Artiklar ba-
serade på Religionsarkeologiska nätverksgruppens
konferens på Lövstadbruk den 1 – 3 december 1995.*
Riksantikvarieämbetet, Arkeologiska undersökningar, Skrifter 19. Linköping.

Hasselmo, M. 1982. *Vadstena*. Riksantikvarieämbetets
och Statens historiska museer rapport: Medeltidsstaden 36. Stockholm.

Hasselmo, M. 1983. *Skänninge*. Riksantikvarieämbetets
och Statens historiska museer rapport: Medeltidsstaden 40. Stockholm.

Helmfrid, S. 1962. *Östergötland Västanstång. Studien
über die ältere Agrarlandschaft und ihre Genese.*
Meddelanden från Geografiska institutionen vid
Stockholms universitet 140. Stockholm.

Kaliff, A. *Arkeologi i Östergötland. Scener ur ett land-
skaps förhistoria.* Occasional Papers in Archaeology
20. 1999. Uppsala.

Klackenberg, H. 1984. *Hästholmen*. Riksantikvarieämbetets och Statens historiska museer rapport:
Medeltidsstaden 59. Stockholm.

Lindeblad, K. Borgs socken – förändringar i tid och
rum 200 – 1200 e Kr. In Lundqvist, L., Lindeblad,
K., Nielsen, A.-L., and Ersgård, L. (eds.), *Slöinge
och Borg. Stormansgårdar i öst och väst.* RAÄ,
Arkeologiska undersökningar, Skrifter 18. Linköping.

Lindeblad, K. 1997. The Town and the Three Farms.
On the Organization of the Landscape in and around
a Medieval Town. In Andersson, H., Carelli, P., and
Ersgård, L. (eds.), *Visions of the Past. Trends and
Traditions in Swedish Medieval Archaeology.* Lund
Studies in Medieval Archaeology 19. RAÄ, Arkeo-
logiska undersökningar, Skrifter 24. Stockholm.

Lindeblad, K. 2001. Motala – en medeltida central-
ort? In Andrén, A., Ersgård, L., Wienberg, J. (eds.),
*Från stad till land. En medeltidsarkeologisk resa
tillägnad Hans Andersson.* Lund Studies in Medieval Archaeology 29. Stockholm.

Lindgren-Hertz, L. 1997. Farm and Landscape. Variations on a Theme in Östergötland. In Andersson,
H., Carelli, P., and Ersgård, L. (eds.), *Visions of
the Past. Trends and Traditions in Swedish Medieval Archaeology.* Lund Studies in Medieval Archaeology 19. RAÄ, Arkeologiska undersökningar, Skrifter 24. Stockholm.

Lindgren-Hertz, L. 2001. Speglingar av rumslig organisation. Norrköping i ljuset av mindre arkeologiska undersökningar. In Andrén, A., Ersgård, L.,
Wienberg, J. (eds.), *Från stad till land. En medeltidsarkeologisk resa tillägnad Hans Andersson.* Lund
Studies in Medieval Archaeology 29. Stockholm.

Lovén, C. 1990. Slotten och de befästa gårdarna i
västra Östergötland. In Dahlbäck, G. (ed.), *I Heliga Birgittas trakter. Nitton uppsatser om medeltida samhälle och kultur i Östergötland "västanstång".* Stockholm.

Neill, T., and Lundberg, S. 1994. Förnyad diskussion
om "Eskilstunakistorna". *Fornvännen* 89.

Nielsen, A.-L. 1996. Borg – enda centralplatsen i Norrköpingsbygden? In Lundqvist, L., Lindeblad, K.,
Nielsen, A.-L., and Ersgård, L. (eds.), *Slöinge och
Borg. Stormansgårdar i öst och väst.* RAÄ, Arkeologiska undersökningar, Skrifter 18. Linköping.

Nilsson, O. 1990. Östergötlands norra bergslager. En
översikt. In Dahlbäck, G. (ed.), *I Heliga Birgittas
trakter. Nitton uppsatser om medeltida samhälle och
kultur i Östergötland "västanstång".* Uppsala.

Tagesson, G. 1997. Who Wants to Live in a Bishop's
Town? On Archaeology and Change in Linköping.
Lund Archaeological Review 1997.

Widgren, M. 1999. Is Landscape History Possible?
Or, How Can We Study the Desertion of Farms?
In Ucko, P. J., and Layton, R. (eds.), *The Archaeo-
logy and Anthropology of Landscape.* London and
New York.

23

Vadstena distinguishes itself in several different ways. Most people associate the town primarily with Saint Birgitta, the patron saint of Europe and perhaps the Swede who is best known outside Sweden, particularly now when the 700th anniversary of her birth is to be celebrated in 2003. Several medieval stone buildings remind us of the town's age of greatness. Besides these there is a largely intact street grid from the fifteenth century, which gives the town its special character. It created a great sensation in the 1950s when a documentation of the masonry in the convent revealed that it consisted of the former palace of the royal estate. This 55-metre-long thirteenth-century building has no counterpart in Scandinavia and is thus a major tourist attraction, together with the convent church and King Gustav Vasa's castle. Thanks to Vadstena convent, the town moreover occupies a special position as regards extant medieval documents.

Vadstena has been the subject of a large number of archaeological investigations. These have mostly

Fig. 1. The seal of the town of Vadstena, from 1417, depicting Saint Birgitta. Photo: National Archives.

Fig. 2. Vadstena viewed from the west. In the foregroun is the castle built by King Gustav Vasa, starting in 1545. To the left is Lake Vättern, the second largest lake in Sweden, bounded by the provinces of Småland, Västergötland, Närke, and Östergötland. Further back in the picture one can see the convent church sticking up, and to the right the remains of St Peter's church, the Red Tower. The medieval neighbourhood of Sanden was in the area on the picture which is concealed by the trees round the castle. Photo: Jan Norrman, RAÄ.

studied trenches dug for pipelines, but there have also been some major excavations. One of the largest in terms of area was conducted in 1995 – 96 at the sixteenth-century castle. If two earlier excavations are included, a total area of some 10,000 m² of the late medieval neighbourhood of Sanden has been excavated. The buildings here were demolished in 1544 to make way for the planned castle. About ten townyards and two streets, one on either side of the townyards, could thus be documented. The large excavation area makes the material rather unique. It has been possible to document the layout of several townyards and study them in their entirety. It has thereby also been possible to compare the settlement patterns and use of several different plots. In addition, the two streets, one of which was a back street, could be studied in detail and in relation to the adjacent townyards. The brief existence of settlement here, from the first half of the fifteenth century until 1544, also makes the material special. Based on this material, I shall paint a picture of late medieval settlement and the layout of the townyards. To begin with I have chosen to describe the landscape and the preconditions for the emergence of the town.

The Vadstena plain

Vadstena is in the western part of Östergötland, on the shore of the large Lake Vättern. This part of the province is one of the biggest wholly cultivated areas in Sweden. The fertile plain has of course been of great significance for the growth of Vadstena. The strategic location on the plain, with the mining district just to the north, meant that place became important in trade with grain and iron ore. Vadstena's position on a bay in the lake made it a good place for the distribution of commodities between Östergötland, Västergötland, Närke, and Småland. Being near the waterside, with the possibility of building a harbour, was probably crucial for the localization of the place.

Vadstena, together with the medieval town of Hästholmen to the south and the medieval central place Motala to the north, are the only ecclesiastical sites on the shore in the area. This presumably reflects their special function and distinctiveness in relation to the surrounding places. The plain around Vadstena is characterized by small parishes with very early churches. Several of the stone churches are dated to the start of the twelfth century, but they were no doubt preceded by wooden churches in the eleventh century, as indi-

Fig. 3. Klåstad round church in the present-day Klosterstad, 4 km east of Vadstena. The church, which was destroyed by the Danes in the Nordic Seven Years War in 1567, showed several medieval features in the interior. The font was to the west along the church's central axis. In this part of the church there were also traces of a lord's gallery of wood. Running along the round wall was a bench as far as the two side altars by the chancel arch. The church consisted of a round nave with an opening in the south-west where a secondary porch built of wood has also been found. The chancel was semicircular. No traces of a sacristy were found north of the chancel. A few metres north of the church, postholes and wall trenches from an eleventh-century church were discovered. Photo: Rikard Hedvall, RAÄ.

cated by, for instance, grave monuments with runic inscriptions in Viking Age style. In several cases the churches are interpreted as having been built by aristocratic families and the king on their estates. At one of these estates, Klosterstad, an archaeological project is in progress, investigating a formerly unknown round church. It was probably erected in the twelfth century or by the start of the thirteenth century at the latest. Just a few metres north of the round church, traces of a stave church have been discovered. A total excavation of this is planned for autumn 2002. A coin from one of the graves, which was struck in the 1030s or 1040s, gives a probable dating of the stave church to the first half of the eleventh century. From the early church we also have about twenty fragments of grave monuments in Viking Age style which can also be dated to the eleventh century. We know from the oldest written evidence about Klosterstad that the estate was owned in 1296 by two of the most distinguished families in the country.

Early remains in the Vadstena district

There are only a few indications of earlier settlement in what was to become the town of Vadstena. Some objects from the Stone Age and Bronze Age have been interpreted as stray finds. The few cemeteries or graves, mostly from the Early Iron Age, are found a little way out of the town.

At the end of the eighteenth century a gold bracteate, dated to the Migration Period, was found in the ground at Vadstena (Brate 1915, p. 167). Gold bracteates are very rare in Scandinavia. In Sweden they have virtually only been found in hoards interpreted as votive deposits. Bracteates then often occur together with other objects of gold, silver, and glass, indications of an elite environment (Andrén 1991, p. 246).

A runestone which stands today in the convent churchyard is also an indication that there was earlier settlement in the area. In the eighteenth century the stone was lying on the shore of Vättern, and it probably originally stood somewhere nearby (Brate 1915, p. 172). Unfortunately, the uncertain details of the

location are typical of ancient monuments and finds in the area, as a result of which the prehistory of the area is in part unknown. The main explanation for this is the cultivation of the surrounding land. One can nevertheless gain hints of the special position of Vadstena in the area right from the Early Iron Age.

Early records speak of the church of Vadstena as a "village church" or a "peasant church". Towards the end of the Middle Ages it is recorded as being dedicated to St Peter (Fröjmark 1990, p. 144). St Peter's is also the name of the parish in which Vadstena was the biggest of several villages. Several of these villages have now vanished.

Vadstena estate
- the royal manor of the Folkunga dynasty

Vadstena was probably no exception to the pattern of magnates' farms with early private churches in Östergötland. Investigation of St Peter's church, the former village church, have resulted in the discovery of walls from an early medieval church. It was north of the Red Tower, which is the only one of the late medieval church buildings to have survived after the demolition at the start of the nineteenth century (Hasselmo 1982, p. 13).

From 1268 we have a charter for Vadstena estate issued by Earl Birger's brother Elof (of the Folkunga dynasty). Further records in the documents testify that the dynasty had a royal manor in Vadstena. A record from the end of the fourteenth century states that King Valdemar was the builder and that the estate was not crown property; in other words, it must have been the king's private property (Fritz 2000, p. 59). The location of the estate was long unknown, but investigations of the masonry in the Birgittine convent in the 1950s and 1960s revealed a 55-metre-long palatial brick building under the plaster on the north wing. It is interpreted as the main building of the royal manor from the mid-thirteenth century. A further five stone houses belonging to the royal manor were discovered in the adjacent buildings. Remains of buildings older than these houses from the royal manor were also found together with a coin of the English king Æthelred II from the period 1009 – 1017 (Anderson 1972, p. 179). These are probably the remains of an older farm. It was presumably as an estate church that the Romanesque church was built in the twelfth century.

The ridge where the church and the Vadstena estate were located must also have been the site of the village, or at least parts of it, known from written sources. There have been few excavations in this part of the town, which might explain why no remains antedating the town have been found here.

The leading cultural institution in Scandinavia - the Birgittine convent

According to a will from 1346, King Magnus Eriksson and Queen Blanka of Namur donated Vadstena estate with the intention of founding a convent. A very important factor for the donation seems to have been the royal burial place established in the middle of the chancel of the convent church. The church would thereby be the last resting place of the Folkunga dynasty (Fritz 2000, pp. 62 ff.).

The site of Saint Birgitta's convent and monastery was consecrated at the end of the 1360s, and in 1384 the convent was formally established (Fritz 2000, pp. 72 ff.). With the establishment of the convent, a town began to grow up around it. The convent, which owned the land where the town was built, was to be of tremendous significance for the existence of the town. Apart from the fact that the place was in a fertile agricultural area and was an important junction for trade, Vadstena now became, above all, a powerful ecclesiastical centre. In addition, the convent was to be Sweden's main cultural institution in the Late Middle Ages. An important factor in this was the men in the monastery who had been educated at Uppsala or on the continent. Their task was to communicate their knowledge to the sixty nuns and their abbess, and to produce literature by copying manuscripts. The library in Vadstena was to be the biggest in Scandinavia, comparable to the biggest libraries in Europe. The majority of the country's extant medieval litera-

ture in Swedish was written in the monastery. The most productive and famous writer was Peder Månsson (Lindroth 1975, pp. 175 ff.). His literary works range from books about art and medicine to manuals on the art of making gold.

Settlement expansion

Before the town received its charter in 1400, those who came on pilgrimage to the convent had to find food for themselves and care for their horses in the village of Starby, south-west of Vadstena (Fritz 2000, p. 84). From 1400 on, when Vadstena had formally become a town, the Urban Law of King Magnus Eriksson applied here, as in the other medieval towns of Sweden.

In the Middle Ages Vadstena differed from the rest of the Hundred of Aska by virtue of its distinctive administrative position. As a hereditary royal possession, Vadstena estate was not subject to the local administration of the crown. The situation was the same after the estate became monastic property. Shortly after Vadstena had received its borough charter, the convent was granted the crown's revenues from the town. The convent leased out the plots, with hereditary right of occupation, while the houses on the plots were privately owned. The town bailiff was appointed by the abbess and the convent, who thereby had a great influence over the government of Vadstena (Fritz 2000, pp. 182 ff.). This of course set its stamp on the town, which made it special in Sweden at the time.

Already in 1382 a person is described as a burgher (Hasselmo 1982, p. 11), which must mean that denser settlement was growing up. Data in written sources from 1428 onwards about "the fosse" can be associated with the excavation results from the Sanden area. A ditch 0.5 m deep and 4–5 m wide was found in the western moat area at the castle. The ditch, which is interpreted as the fosse around the town, can be dated to the end of the fourteenth century or the start of the fifteenth century (Hedvall in prep.).

Documentary information that the fosse also extended close to the hospital, the convent, and a bishop's

Fig. 4. The Birgittine convent in Vadstena, formerly the royal manor of the Folkunga dynasty from the mid-thirteenth century. Photo: Pål-Nils Nilsson.

estate allow us to estimate the area of the town as 17 ha. We thus know that its growth was almost explosive. From the establishment of the convent and for the coming 20 – 50 years, the whole stretch of land along Lake Vättern to the castle area, almost a kilometre away, was already built up. When the inhabitants in the 1460s were granted permission by the convent to dig a new fosse around the town, its area was doubled.

The plots

The town of Vadstena, as we have seen, was built on land owned by Vadstena convent. The convent stated as the standard dimensions of a building plot that it should be 21.6 m long and 16.2 m wide, including eaves. The lease for a plot was half a Swedish mark and twelve days of corvée a year (Fritz 2000, p. 182). A quick look through the medieval written sources does not show any uniformity as regards the size and appearance of the plots. None of them is said to have measured the same as the standard dimensions stated by the convent. Within the fosse and moat there were not only built plots but also gardens, kaleyards, stables, and byres. The oldest list of Vadstena's taxpayers from 1560 states the number of taxable households as 237; there were 190 house plots, 12 stables and byres on separate plots, 140 gardens and kaleyards, including kaleyards outside the town itself. The number of independent plots was 342 (Söderström 2000, p. 320).

The Sanden area

The present blocks of Asylen, Slottsparken, and Slottet together made up the Sanden area (see fig. 5). Also belonging to this was the urban settlement south-west of the castle, although we do not know where the boundary on this side ran (Hedvall 1996, p. 22). The neighbourhood was not densely built in the earliest phase. Dendrochronological dates from house planks and dates on coins indicate that this area was first settled in the first half of the fifteenth century. Before houses could be built, a marshy area on the landward side, in the present southern moat area, was filled with earth. This was a common practice in Vadstena in the Middle Ages, and well into modern times, to acquire more land for buildings. By reclaiming land from Lake Vättern, for example, the neighbouring blocks of Slottsvakten and Slottsherren have had their area tripled until the present day (Hedvall 1994a, p. 19). The park in front of the castle gives an incorrect picture of the former topography. In actual fact, the waters of Vättern originally reached the castle. Extensive filling in connection with the building of the castle, and in particular the construction of the harbour piers and the park in the nineteenth century, have completely changed this picture (Hedvall 1994b, p. 74).

Contact with the water was of great significance, as was the case in other medieval towns located on shores. This is revealed by a recurrent pattern in the plot structure of the towns. The plots were long and narrow, extending from the water towards land. In this way, most plots had direct contact with the water, where there were opportunities for fishing, washing, having one's own jetty, and fetching water.

Inhabitants and activities in Sanden

Few early references to the Sanden area are known; the oldest is dated 2 June 1493. Because of the expropriation of property for construction of the castle, however, there are fuller written sources. For the first eviction of 1544, which affected 30 townyards, 27 persons are named in King Gustav Vasa's accounts, with no statement as to whether they own or just occupy the properties. Many of the townyards were owned by big farmers who only lived there occasionally (Fritz 2000, p. 181), for example, when they wanted to attend special masses in the convent church or carry out transactions at the market. When the owner was not in the town, the property was managed by a steward. Of the names or townyards that are mentioned, the following can be associated with a trade or a special use: kaleyards, Antonius Smed (smith), Jon Beltare (belt-maker), Lars Koppslagare (copper-smith), byre, and Pungmakare (purse-maker). Contemporary records also note that townyards were owned or used by King Gustav Vasa, noblemen, the convent, craftsmen, and a widow (Unnerbäck 1963, p. 116). Some of these can be linked to the archaeological material.

A pot-founder worked on plot 9. An interesting name in Gustav Vasa's list, which may have been connected with foundry work, is Jon the belt-maker. His work could be complex. It is obvious from the name that he worked with belts and other articles of leather, but he may also have cast the buckles and mountings. Moreover, the belt-maker is sometimes referred to as a pot-founder (Norberg 1981, pp. 30 ff.). Much of townyard no. 9 is covered with slag and moulds for three-footed pots. The material of some of the pieces of slag consists of amalgams of lead, zinc, antimony, arsenic, cobalt, nickel, and copper. This composition evokes the experimental zeal of an alchemist. Both antimony and arsenic, moreover, are typical alchemical elements. Another interesting thing in this context is the occurrence of nickel and cobalt, which were not discovered until the middle of the eighteenth century (Kresten 1997, p. 113). Since the different types of slag and the moulds were lying together, one may assume that the same person who cast the pots also experimented with the other metals.

Plot 2 yielded a large volume of material, including iron slag. Perhaps this is a residue of the work of Antonius the smith, as the leather waste on plot 6 could be the scant remains of the purse-maker in Sanden. Other craftsmen pursued their trades in the area.

Fig. 5. Town plan of Vadstena. The Sanden area consisted of the blocks of Asylen, Slottsparken, and Slottet. The Red Tower is the only surviving part of the late medieval church of St Peter. Immediately to the north of this, parts of a Romanesque church have been found on several occasions. At least part of the medieval village must have been on the ridge with Skänningegatan, St Peter's church, and the royal manor (later the convent). The extant medieval buildings, excavated foundations of stone houses, and stone houses known from archival sources are marked on the map. Graphics: Lars Östlin, RAÄ.

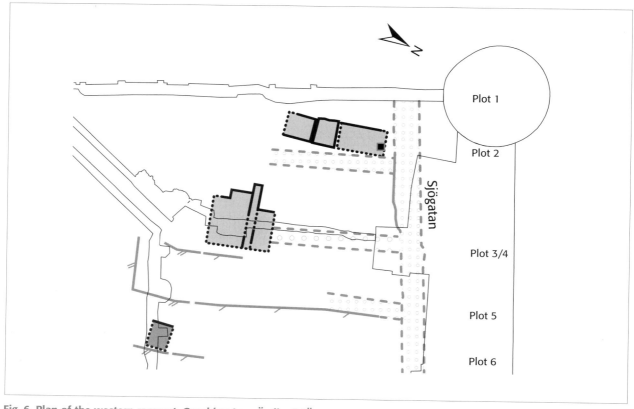

Plot 1

Plot 2

Sjögatan

Plot 3/4

Plot 5

Plot 6

Fig. 6. Plan of the western rampart. Graphics: Lars Östlin, RAÄ.

A great deal of wrongly fired pottery was found, above all in the older excavations of the courtyard on plot 8. A potter in Master Sten's yard in Sanden is known from 1541. It was in all probability townyard no. 8 that was owned by Sten. It is said to be adjacent to one of Gustav Vasa's own townyards (Unnerbäck 1963, p. 114). Perhaps it was townyard no. 7 that the king owned. The buildings here differed from those on other plots. The whole plot was built, and one of the houses was of stone.

The excavated bones, as analysed by Barbro Hårding, show that cattle were the most common species of animal in the townyards in Sanden. Above all, people kept older cows, which indicates an economy based on milk products. The picture is the same for sheep and goat, the next largest category of bone. Among the slaughtering waste, however, pigs were

the most common species. This can give us an idea of the stock of animals in a townyard. Fish bones are another large group, accounting for 20 per cent of the bones, which is not strange for a place on Lake Vättern, yet it noteworthy that a fifth of the fish bones come from sea species. Saltwater fish were thus transported over a long distance to the town (Hårding 2000, pp. 111 ff.).

The oldest townyards

The excavated house remains could be divided into two phases. The oldest houses, from the first half of the fifteenth century until a fire ravaged the town in 1487, were more dispersed. The remains of buildings consist of rows of sill stones, floor surfaces of wood, brick, and stone, fireplace foundations of stone and brick, along with cobbled streets and alleys. The long, narrow townyards in Sanden reached 60 – 70 m in towards land from the street named Sjögatan, which ran along the lake. The width of most plots was just over 10 metres.

The two oldest townyards which could be excavated in their entirety showed different layouts. One had some smaller houses in a row from Sjögatan and some distance into the plot, no. 2 (see fig. 6). In the middle of the fifteenth century the houses were moved further into the plots. During the hundred years when the townyard was occupied, smithing was carried on here, as shown by a large amount of slag and several iron blanks. Originally the ironworking must have been done at one of the hearths closest to Sjögatan. Metal craft in the area right beside the street is also attested in other parts of the town in both archaeological and written evidence. Several other craft furnaces/hearths in Sanden were in this location, albeit in a later phase. This indicates a pattern with craft activity at the front of the plots, very close to the streets. The finds from the oldest phase of plot 2 have no pottery. This suggests that the property was not inhabited, serving only as craft premises where forging was done. Hearth foundations and floors of clay and stone likewise indicate that this was not a dwelling.

The other plot, no. 3/4, had no building along Sjögatan (see fig. 6). The house, and slightly later two houses, stood roughly in the centre of the plot. An alley led from the houses to Sjögatan. The function of the big building on the plot is uncertain. A rebuilding layer

Fig. 7. Bakery on plot 8, with a large brick oven in one corner. In the room outside the oven door the floor was stone-paved. In the other part of the house there was a wooden floor. The joists on which the floor planks rested were placed on top of the five stones in this part (a sixth stone was dug away when the round well was dug in the twentieth century). Photo: RAÄ.

in the house contained various finds indicating an ordinary household. One problem is that the whole building was not excavated, so we do not know whether there was a hearth and if so what it looked like. In size and appearance, the building is different from what was found on the neighbouring plot. A comparison of the finds likewise shows great dissimilarities, illustrating the different activities in the two townyards. For instance, there is copious pottery on plot 3/4.

Further in on several of the plots, behind the buildings, were the kaleyards. Great amounts of earth had been spread early on in these parts, probably when the kaleyards were first established. They were cultivated until the eviction in 1544. The traces of cultivation show that the earth was worked with spades. Marks of spade points were visible in the sand under the topsoil. These were found sparsely over large areas and also more concentrated in long, narrow bed-like constellations. Macrofossil analyses show that the kaleyards were used for growing parsnip, flax, and other plants. The townyards were bounded at the back by a street laid out in the mid-fifteenth century. Along this back street there were in several cases outbuildings of a simple kind marking the limit of the kaleyards. In one case there was a better-built bakery. Another building was interpreted as a stable or byre. The animal houses may have been on the back street because it was easy to take the animals out of the yard, for example, when they were driven to pasture. There was thus no need for the animals to cross the yard. In this back region there were also latrines. To give some privacy, a few of them had been screened off with one or two simple walls.

Regulated plots

Boundary markers were found between the plots. They consisted primarily of ditches, 20 – 30 cm deep and wide. The ditches have only been documented in the unbuilt back sections of the plots, close to the back street. Towards the front of the plots, the boundaries were instead marked by buildings and alleys. In a few cases the boundary was also marked with a row of bigger stones in the street paving, which could also differ from one plot to another. In subsequent phases the ditches were succeeded by wattle fences, which in some cases were finally replaced by sturdy posts, which are interpreted as having borne plank fences. It was difficult to follow this process of change, so it is not easy to say to which phase the different types of fence belong. It is at least clear that the trenches belong to the earliest phase and the posts to the latest. Some posts in the fence have been dendrochronologically dated to 1498.

The later townyards

A great change took place when the townyards were rebuilt after the fire in 1487 (see fig. 8). Only two houses survived the fire. In the western moat area the burnt remains of the older buildings were covered with large layers of levelling soil. The new buildings were erected on these, much more densely than before the fire.

The structural change was equally noticeable. Suddenly there were no less than six houses with fireplaces as against the few that had previously existed. The buildings seem to have constituted a stable picture, with a row of houses along a cobbled alley running from Sjögatan into the plot. The alley was the main entrance to the townyard. The number of houses on the plot varied between 3 and 7. In the parts closer to Sjögatan, where few remains of buildings were found, the houses were presumably simpler.

Along the main street, Storgatan, the convent owned in principle all the shops. They were let by the convent and did not necessarily have any connection with the lessee of the plot behind the shop. The shops are stated in the cadastre of Vadstena convent to be 3.2 by 4.3 m in size (Söderström 2000, pp. 224 ff.). Sjögatan was probably also lined with these shops.

Behind the shop on several plots, there were buildings with ovens or simple hearths. Several of them were small and round. In some cases there were thick layers of soot and ashes beside the fireplaces in the outbuildings, a feature not found at the fireplaces in the dwelling houses. Other buildings in this part and further in on the plots which had no hearths can be interpreted as stores.

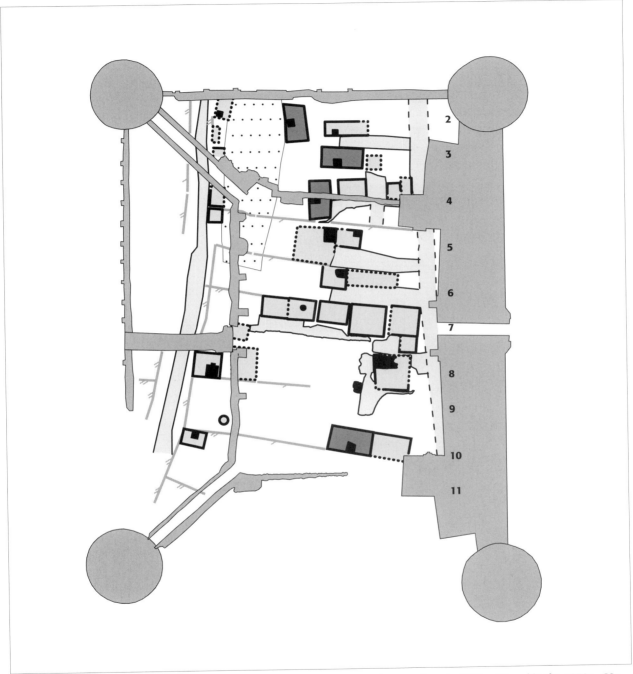

Fig. 8. Reconstruction of settlement 1487–1544 on the basis of the results of excavations in 1995 – 96 and in the 1950s –60s. The numbers mark the different plots. Key to colours: black – hearths, grey – the castle, dark grey – dwelling houses, light grey – other buildings, grey line – fences, light area with dots – kaleyards, black circle – a well, and light grey – streets and alleys. Graphics: Lars Östlin, RAÄ.

Furthest in from the street in the row of houses was the dwelling house. The location in the middle of the property created a division into a front yard and a back yard. In some cases the dwelling house was built across the plot, at right angles to the other houses in the row. The back yard may be seen as the private part, while the front yard was more for public show. In some instances there are traces of cobbling in the front yard. Behind the dwelling house, as far as the back street, there was still the kaleyard and privy. This part of the townyard constituted a private space. From the 1480s there was a sturdy fence between it and the back street. At the same time fences were put up between the plots, which presumably kept inquisitive neighbours from seeing into the back yard. Besides giving privacy to people going to the toilet, the fence may also have been built to prevent the theft of vegetables from the kaleyard and to keep out animals.

Fig. 9. Dwelling house on plot 2, from the end of the fifteenth century. The plan seems to represent a completely new idea of what a home should look like. The house type caught on immediately in Sanden. The square assemblage of stone is the hearth foundation. To the right of this is the living room with its wooden floor. There could also be earth-filled benches along the sides of this room. On the other side of the hearth, the house was divided into two small rooms. One of these was the porch, which usually had a brick floor (parts of which can be seen to the top left). The room behind it could have been a chamber or a store. Photo: RAÄ.

There must also have been a way out to the back street, through the fence or through a house. That would have been an easy way to drive the animals stabled in the houses along the back street. Roughly half of the houses along the street had a small hearth foundation. On plot 9 there was a well in this back room, the only room discovered by the excavation.

Dwelling houses following the plan of the "single house" (*enkelstuga*), consisting of one all-purpose room plus a porch and a little chamber, seem to have caught on in the town after the fire. This house type, and the position of the dwelling a good way in from the street, was customary in the town at least until the end of the sixteenth century, as other excavations have shown.

Some of the dwelling houses were shown to have been built of corner-jointed logs, which was presumably the universally prevailing building technique. They consisted of a wooden-floored living room running in the longitudinal direction of the house, surrounding the hearth on two sides. In a few cases there was evidence of *mullbänkar*, banks of earth and stone filling running along the bottom of the walls, to insulate against draughts and simultaneously serve as benches. The other part of the house consisted of one or two small rooms. One of these was the porch, which in several cases had a floor of limestone, brick, or stones. In the latter half of the sixteenth century the floor of the porch had in many cases been replaced by a wooden one. The entrance was towards one corner of the house, on the side facing the alley. Behind the porch was a small room with an earth floor or perhaps a wooden floor, possibly used as a store or a chamber. The fireplace, which was always on the side opposite the entrance, was large and solid. Occasionally the foundation was almost a metre high, consisting of 4 – 5 courses of stone. The foundation probably bore a chimney. The hearths in the dwelling houses ranged in size from 2 by 3 m to 1.2 by 1.4. The hearths in the dwelling houses were much larger and more solid than in the houses that are interpreted as outbuildings, apart from certain ovens.

If one looks at the townyards that have been excavated in their entirety, one can see that that the layout did not differ noticeably after the fire of 1487. The main difference concerns how much of the plot was built up. Regardless of how many houses the townyard had, the dwelling house was located roughly in the middle of the plot. An exception is plot 7, where virtually the whole area of the plot was built up. It did not have the type of dwelling house described above. Instead, the dwelling was probably in the stone house which was retracted from the street. Of course, there were also plots in the town which were used as gardens or byres where there were no houses or no more than a single building.

The finds in the houses often proved difficult to interpret. This may be due to the movements of soil that have taken place on the plots. Apart from the large levelling layers that were spread, small foundations were also laid for the houses. Often things like horseshoe nails are found inside the houses in layers which must in part have been deposited during the time when the house was used. A large proportion of the finds probably derives from activities in the houses. A common category of find in the living room is a coin or two. Another large body of finds from the houses includes details for doors and windows, such as hasps, handles, hinges, locks, and keys. Furniture details consist of objects such as mountings and handles for chests, candleholders, and parts of wrought-iron chandeliers or candlesticks.

Great upheavals in Vadstena in the sixteenth century

With the Reformation in 1527, Vadstena convent declined in significance, although the last nuns did not leave the convent until 1595. The whole town started to decline soon afterwards. The year 1544 was moreover a fateful one for Udd Knutsson, Nils Uggle, Tolstad-Lasse, and all the other inhabitants of Sanden. The Diet of Västerås decided in that year that one of the new national castles was to be built in Vadstena. This meant a new upswing for the town after

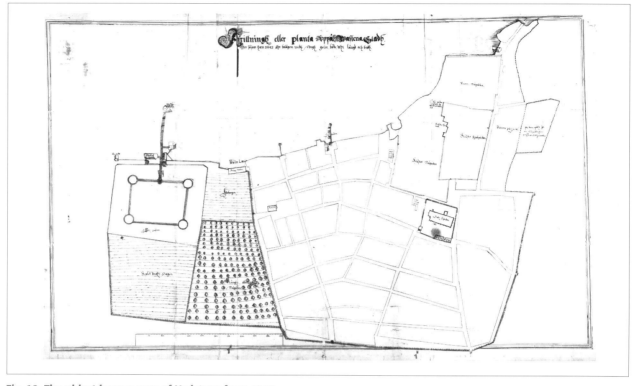

Fig. 10. The oldest known map of Vadstena from 1642.

the Reformation. For the people living in Sanden, however, the decision meant an end to their life in that neighbourhood. The inhabitants were assigned other plots in the town or elsewhere. Some plots were bought up for cash. The decision must also have been a great event in the history of Vadstena, which probably left its traces in the whole town. An entire neighbourhood, with an estimated hundred townyards, was evacuated. The area affected corresponded to 20 – 25 per cent of the town's built-up area. The result must have been much denser settlement in the other parts of the town. Vehement protests were heard from other townspeople who were urged to give up land to the evicted people. Unbuilt land previously owned by the convent was also used for buildings now (Hedvall 1999).

A decade or so later, all the structures of the medieval neighbourhood of Sanden had vanished. The oldest map of the town, from 1642, shows no traces of the streets, the bakery, Lord Sten's large property, or Antonius' forge.

For the rest of the town the situation was different. Today's street grid agrees to a large extent with the medieval layout. Even the plot structure is in many cases the same. Thanks to the excavation in Sanden we now also know the layout of several townyards in the Late Middle Ages. Apart from the preserved medieval structure of the urban space, there are also a large number of houses surviving from the Middle Ages. These consist of, for instance, the town hall, the hospital, several shops, and the previously mentioned royal manor and the convent. Altogether, this makes Vadstena very special among the medieval towns of Sweden.

■ **Rikard Hedvall**

References

Anderson, I. 1972. *Vadstena gård och kloster*. Uppsala.

Andrén, A. 1991. Guld och makt – en tolkning av de skandinaviska guldbrakteaternas funktion. In Fabech, C., and Ringtved, J. (eds.), *Samfundsorganistion og Regional Variation. Norden i romersk jernalder og folkevandringstid. Beretning fra 1. nordiske jernaldersymposium på Sandbjerg Slot 11 – 15 april 1989*. Jysk Arkæologisk Selskabs Skrifter XXVII. Århus.

Brate, E. 1915. *Östergötlands runinskrifter. Sveriges runinskrifter 2*. Stockholm.

Fritz, B. 2000. [Section on the Middle Ages.] In Söderström. G. (ed.), *600 år i Vadstena*. Stockholm.

Fröjmark, A. 1990. Kyrkornas skyddshelgon i Östergötland "västanstång" under tidig medeltid. In Dahlbäck, G. (ed.), *I Heliga Birgittas trakter. Nitton uppsatser om medeltida samhälle och kultur i Östergötland "västanstång"*. Stockholm.

Hårding, B. 2000. Sanden. En osteologisk undersökning av några stadsgårdar vid Vadstena slott. Osteologisk analysrapport. In Hedvall, R. (ed.), *Stadsgårdar i den senmedeltida stadsdelen Sanden, Vadstena*. Rapport UV Öst 2000:26. Linköping.

Hasselmo, M. 1982. *Vadstena*. Riksantikvarieämbetets och Statens historiska museer rapport: Medeltidsstaden 36. Stockholm.

Hedvall, R. 1994a. *Slottsherren. Arkeologisk förundersökning*. Byrån för arkeologiska undersökningar UV Linköping 1994:19.

Hedvall, R. 1994b. *Vadstena slott, Norra kajen, RAÄ 15. Arkeologisk förundersökning*. Riksantikvarieämbetet Byrån för arkeologiska undersökningar UV Linköping, Linköping 1994:74.

Hedvall, R. 1996. *Vadstena slott, RAÄ 15 och RAÄ 21, Arkeologisk undersökning inför uppförandet av ett brofäste med anslutningsväg på den västra sidan om den västra vallgraven*. Riksantikvarieämbetet, Avdelningen för arkeologiska undersökningar, UV Linköping.

Hedvall, R. 1999. *Äldre bebyggelse i den medeltida stadens östra utkant. Kv Prelaten. Arkeologisk förundersökning*. Rapport UV Öst 1999:30. Linköping.

Hedvall, R. (ed.) 2000. *Stadsgårdar i den senmedeltida stadsdelen Sanden, Vadstena*. Rapport UV Öst 2000:26. Linköping.

Hedvall, R. In prep. Ett byggnadsverk till "värn och tröst" – Vadstenas medeltida stadsbefästning. In *Arkeologi i Vadstena – Nya resultat med utgångspunkt i undersökningarna i stadsdelen Sanden*.

Kresten, P. 2000. Geoarkeologi. Smide och alkemi? Slagger och metaller från Vadstena. Slagganalysrapport. In Hedvall, R. (ed.), *Stadsgårdar i den senmedeltida stadsdelen Sanden, Vadstena*. Rapport UV Öst 2000:26. Linköping.

Lindroth, S. 1975. *Svensk lärdomshistoria. Medeltiden, reformationstiden*. Stockholm.

Norberg, R. 1981. Gördel och gördelmakare. In *Kulturhistoriskt lexikon för nordisk medeltid 6*. Copenhagen.

Söderström, G. (ed.) 2000. *600 år i Vadstena*. Stockholm.

Unnerbäck, E. 1963. Sanden, en medeltida stadsdel i Vadstena. *Meddelanden 1962–1963, Östergötlands och Linköpings stads museum*. Linköping.

Introduction

"Stories say that this town was once a large and distinguished commercial town in Östergötland, and this is indeed likely, for although the town is now small and easy to grasp, around the outside of the town there are nevertheless many oven bases and house foundations in the adjacent plots and fields" (Olsson *et al.* 1969). This record from the seventeenth century describes Skänninge as a town which had previously had considerable workshop activity outside the town centre that we see in the oldest maps.

It is sometimes difficult to determine how much faith to put in early written sources, but the fact is that a building project recently started on the eastern edge of the town has given archaeologists new opportunities to study the growth of the early Skänninge. The project concerns the extension of the railway that runs along the east of Skänninge (fig. 2). The results of the initial investigations suggest that the place had considerable craft activity as early as the eleventh to the thirteenth centuries, with permanent settlement spread over a far wider area than has previously been known. This article will be about these preliminary findings. It will also show how much new and valuable information can be obtained from a seemingly limited archaeological effort. There are many indications that the new findings will partly change our image of the early history of Skänninge.

Skänninge and its hinterland

In an article from 1992, Margareta Hasselmo compiled the archaeological data then existing about early medieval central places in Sweden. Skänninge is one of those early central places which, in her opinion, was part of a system of important central places alongside the early medieval towns of Sigtuna, Visby, Skara, and Gamla Lödöse. A characteristic of these central places was that they were well located for communications, often at points where land and water routes crossed. These early places are also characterized by having gradually grown out of seasonal activities associated with the place, without any true lasting settlement, into permanent and regulated settlements (Hasselmo 1992, p. 50).

Skänninge first stands out as a town in a formal sense in the thirteenth century, situated in the western part of the rich agricultural area of Östergötland. The concentration of settlement in the fertile plains in the centre of the province, from Vättern in the west to the Baltic Sea in the east, is also a characteristic feature of the distribution of both Iron Age and early medieval settlement. Skänninge has been held up as one of the central places in the province as early as the Late Iron Age and the Early Middle Ages. There is a great deal of evidence in the known archaeological material to corroborate this picture, for instance the large number of runestones in the surrounding countryside. In Skänninge and its environs we find about a quarter of the roughly 250 runestones of Östergötland (Hasselmo 1987, p. 239). Further indications of the early central importance of Skänninge and its hinterland come from the rich occurrence of early medieval grave slabs with runic inscriptions, known as Eskilstuna cists. These are generally dated to the mid-eleventh century and are considered to be closely connected to the king and

Fig. 1. The town seal from 1384. Photo: National Archives.

Fig. 2. Aerial photograph taken from the south, showing the whole stretch of land affected by the development. It is planned to widen the railway with yet another track on the east side. Apart from this, the areas where roads and bridges cross the railway will be excavated. Photo from southeast with lake Vättern in the background. Photo: Jan Norrman, RAÄ.

the early Christian mission. The sepulchral monuments are also thought to have been connected to the oldest churches and consecrated burial places (summed up by Lindeblad and Nielsen 2000, p. 163; see also Hedvall, this volume). Recent research has suggested that the churches were early religious centres of a religious and secular nature, where magnates who supported the king chose to be buried (Neill and Lundberg 1994). Archaeological investigations at the town's two medie-val churches have discovered fragments of such sepulchral monuments, which strengthens the image of a place controlled by local magnates' families in the Late Iron Age and Early Middle Ages (Hasselmo 1983; Lindeblad and Nielsen 2000).

Because of its central location in the rich agricultural land, and a well-developed network of roads converging in the town, it is now believed that Skänninge in the Early Middle Ages functioned as a collection

Fig. 3. Our Lady's church, built around 1300, is one of the three medieval churches still surviving in Skänninge. The church is in the centre of the town, beside Stora Torget, which still serves as a market place today. Photo: Pål-Nils Nilsson.

early estates of lords and kings had for the central place and the emergence of the later town. Generally speaking, however, the growth of the early central places in the province is perceived as a process closely connected with an active central power (Hasselmo 1992, p. 50; Ersgård 2000, p.14).

The oldest Skänninge - written sources and earlier archaeological research

Margareta Hasselmo summed up the knowledge that existed in the 1980s about the development of Skänninge from a central place to a town in the eleventh to thirteenth centuries (Hasselmo 1983, 1987). In the article from 1987 she also presents the results of small-scale research excavations. The aim of these investigations was to find traces of settlement which could be associated with the period before the formation of the town. One observation made by Hasselmo was that the source material for the early history of Skänninge at that time was defective and limited. Here I shall briefly outline the earlier source situation and then present the new findings from the excavations of 1999–2000. The results of the ongoing archaeological project are still preliminary, but there is much to suggest that they will change the picture of the early history of the place.

The first time Skänninge is mentioned in written sources is 1178. This is in a tutelary charter issued by Pope Alexander III to the episcopal see of Linköping. In this charter the pope declares his protection of the bishop's seat and its land holdings. Among the property is "a farm beside Skänninge with adjacent lands" (Hasselmo 1983, p. 10). However, the previously mentioned burial monuments have been able to date two of the churches in the town, St Martin's and All Saints, about a hundred years earlier than this, to the eleventh or twelfth century (Lindqvist 1970, p. 134; Cnattingius and Lindahl 1970, p. 25). Fragmentary and uncertain traces of early medieval settlement have also been found beside these two churches. This has been interpreted as indicating that there were large farms near the churches (Hasselmo 1987, p. 251).

place for the surplus agrarian produce of the surrounding countryside (Hasselmo 1987, p. 239). In addition, the River Skenaån flows through the present urban area, linking the place with another medieval town, Linköping. The town grew up in the middle of this rich district, surrounded by magnates' farms and royal estates, such as Bjälbo, Biskopsberga, and Högby. Bjälbo is assumed to have been the main seat of the Folkunga dynasty, and it is yet another place where excavations have found the burial monuments mentioned above. It is not clear what significance these

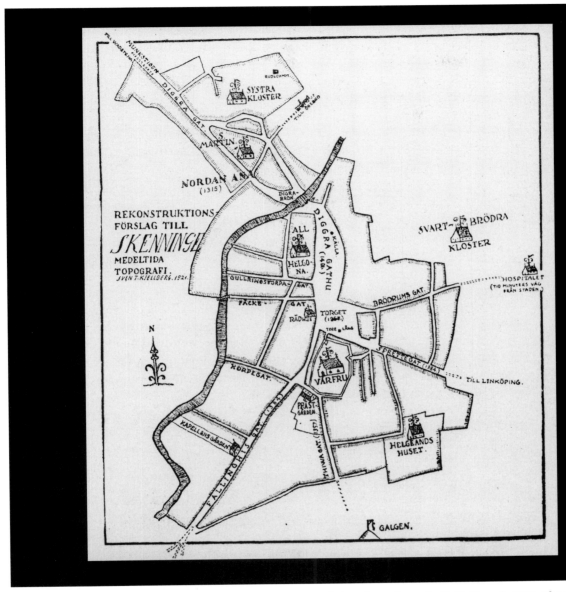

Fig. 4. A suggested reconstruction of the topography of medieval Skänninge, drawn by T. Kjellberg in 1921. The map shows the location of several of the institutions mentioned in medieval written sources. Several of these sites have been partially excavated. Kjellberg placed St Martin's church south of St Ingrid's convent, but research excavations in 1985 noticed remains of walls within the actual convent ruin, which were interpreted as possible remains of the older church (Hasselmo 1987, p. 249). The excavations that have now started cover areas which can be placed just east of St Ingrid's convent in the reconstruction (labelled *systraklostret* on the map). Remains were found here of workshop activities and early medieval settlement. Both north and south of the ruins of St Olaf's friary (*svartbrödraklostret*) there are also remains of workshop activities. It is as yet uncertain whether these should be ascribed to the monastery period or come from the early phase of Skänninge's history. In addition, the excavation takes in an area just east of the House of the Holy Spirit (Helgeandshuset) which is visible in the lower part of the picture. There are traces here of settlement which may be of early medieval date.

By the early thirteenth century Skänninge had taken on an urban character with its two churches, one on either side of the River Skenaån, and with the addition of several new institutions. According to a document from 1280, there was a hospital in Skänninge before 1208, probably the oldest in the country. In 1237 the Dominicans established their second house in Sweden, St Olaf's. The monastery was completely destroyed by a fire in 1291 but was rebuilt in 1305. In the latter part of the thirteenth century and the early fourteenth century the town continued to expand. In 1287 it is stated that there was a mint in the town, and in the decade before this, yet another Dominican house was founded on the northern outskirts of the town, the convent of St Ingrid. This convent was established on the site of the earlier St Martin's church. A third church was erected around 1300, Our Lady's (Hasselmo 1983) (fig. 3). A House of the Holy Spirit is mentioned in written sources for the first time in 1331; it is assumed to have been on the south-east edge of the town, at the present-day railway park (fig. 4).

Between the two monastic houses on the east bank of the Skenaån there are also remains of a presumed castle. This consists of a noticeable height just north-west of the ruins of St Olaf's monastery in Dyhagen, which was previously marshy. An earlier excavation of the hill revealed vitrified medieval brick and remains of masonry. The remains were interpreted as the town's medieval brickworks, mentioned in a source from the end of the fifteenth century (Hasselmo 1983). Another suggested interpretation is that the hill is the remains of the Bishop of Linköping's castle in Skänninge. "Biskopsholman i Skeninge" is mentioned in a document from 1414. The castle could have moved here, away from the large village of Biskopsberga ("Bishop's Hill"), just north of the town (Lovén 1996, pp. 246 ff.). In the marshy parts just east of the hill, various wooden structures and large quantities of animal bones have been found on two occasions. The remains have been interpreted as a bridge and a dam (Hasselmo 1983). These remains should probably be linked to activities on the hill.

Small-scale investigations at different places in the town in the 1980s revealed remains which are older than the medieval urban settlement (Hasselmo 1987; 1992, p. 41). The early remains are confined to an area west of St Martin's church, the crossing of the river at Järntorget, and a larger area, the actual plateau, south of All Saints' church.

On the basis of the limited archaeological material that was known about Skänninge before the formation of the town proper, the following conclusions were drawn:

On the east bank of the Skenaån, beside a ford, limited archaeological investigations have uncovered traces of Viking Age and early medieval deposits which were interpreted as showing that there was a market place in the area.

South of the market place was one of the early medieval churches, All Saints'. Hasselmo has interpreted this as a royal estate church attached to Biskopsberga north of the town. Right beside the church and south of it, a limited amount of highly fragmentary archaeological material has been found, but sufficient to indicate the existence of settlement in the area in the oldest phase of the church's history in the eleventh century.

On the other side of the river, by the other early medieval church, St Martin's, excavations have shown that there were contemporary buildings beside the church. The interpretation of this is that the church belonged to a magnate's farm (Hasselmo 1987, p. 251) (fig. 5).

The excavations of 1999 – 2000

As shown by Hasselmo's compilation of 1987, no major excavations have been conducted in Skänninge, and there is very limited archaeological material that can be associated with the period before the emergence of Skänninge as a town in the true sense. However, the project now started, as a result of plans by the National Rail Administration to expand the railway, has given archaeology new opportunities to study the growth of Skänninge from a central place in the Late Iron Age/Early Middle Ages to a fully developed medie-

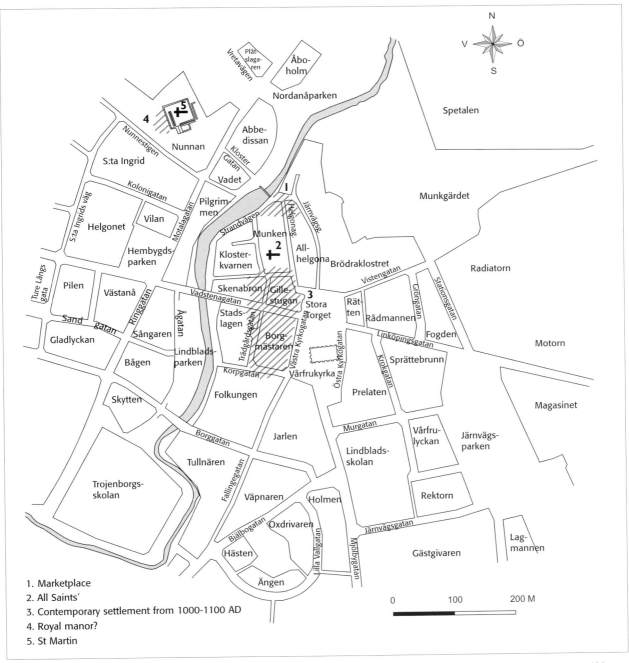

1. Marketplace
2. All Saints'
3. Contemporary settlement from 1000-1100 AD
4. Royal manor?
5. St Martin

Fig. 5. The map shows an earlier suggestion as to the distribution of settlement in Skänninge in the eleventh and twelfth centuries, based on the archaeological data known at the time. Around the two early medieval churches, St Martin's west of the river and All Saints' east of the river, traces of contemporary settlement have been found (the hatched sections), for which the interpretation is that there were large farms beside these churches. Remains of a presumed earlier market place have been found in the hatched area closest to the river. After Hasselmo 1987, p. 250. Graphics: Lars Östlin, RAÄ.

val town in the course of the thirteenth century. The planned railway will affect a stretch roughly 1 km long through the eastern outskirts of Skänninge. This part of the town has seen relatively little research hitherto.

The results of the initial investigations show remains which shed fascinating new light on the early history of Skänninge. Among other things, the excavations revealed remains from the Late Iron Age/Early Middle Ages, thick deposits with remains of settlement, and craft waste. The planned excavations also take in St Olaf's monastery, the monastic outbuildings, and the eastern border of the town.

Traces of settlement and a market place - the early central place?

Results of earlier excavations have led archaeologists to locate an early market place at the crossing of the river between the two oldest churches. It has also been possible to associate contemporary settlement with the area around these churches. The excavations commenced in 1999, however, suggest that permanent settlement and a workshop/market site covered a much larger area than the earlier archaeological evidence indicated.

Less than 100 m east of St Martin's church and the ruins of St Ingrid's convent, discoveries included the remains of a building and an occupation layer 0.3 m thick. The building was dated to the Early Middle Ages through finds of early black earthenware. At the same time as the National Heritage Board's excavations, some small trenches were dug west of the excavation in Motalagatan (see fig. 5). Here too, deposits with Viking Age/early medieval finds were noted (Björkhager, in prep.). The layers thus seem to be part of a continuous early medieval activity zone running at least from Järntorget for a further 200 m or more to the north-east, to a workshop area on the west bank of the Skenaån.

In the area with the workshop activities there was a layer with waste from the manufacture of combs of antler and bone, as well as comb blanks of bone and bronze wire for the rivets. Iron slag also indicates metal manufacture on the site (fig. 6). Besides the layer with craft waste there were also a large number of postholes and large, oblong, pit-like features which may be traces of sunken-floor huts or house cellars. Parts of a sunken-floor hut were also excavated in the area. Sunken-floor huts, which often occur at Viking Age market centres, are usually associated with crafts, and common finds are, for example, spindle whorls; this is also the case in the present hut.

The pottery uncovered by the initial excavation gives a good basis for dating, with finds of black earthenware indicating that the area may possibly have been first occupied in the eleventh century or the early twelfth century. Pottery from previous excavations in Skänninge has been analysed by Mats Roslund, who believes that most of the pottery is of domestic manufacture. The forms are based on a Scandinavian Viking Age tradition and not, as formerly believed, on Wendish influences (Roslund 2001, p. 198). Earlier excavations at St Martin's church have previously yielded early medieval pottery, which was probably imported. The pots from this area have clear parallels in Russian pottery and can be dated to the twelfth century or the early thirteenth (ibid., p. 198).

The southward extent of the central place

An area about 600 m south of the concentration of settlement that we glimpse around the two early churches is interesting in this connection. In the present-day railway park just east of the House of the Holy Spirit, part of a layer containing prehistoric or early medieval pottery, animal bones, and cracked stone was excavated (see fig. 4). This further increases the extent of the oldest activity area in Skänninge. We are still not sure what this layer represents. The occurrence of cracked stone and the thickness of the layer, up to 0.3 m, nevertheless indicates the proximity of settlement: if so, it is a different type not associated with craft activities.

On the other side of the railway there was a deposit with several strata with a total thickness of 0.5 m. Once again there were finds of craft waste. Sawn bone

Fig. 6. Objects found in the area of workshop activities on the west bank of the River Skenaån. The picture shows parts of combs and bronze wire for riveting the parts together. Residue from comb manufacture was also found in the form of ends of cattle joints. Iron slag shows that forging was also carried on at the site. Photo: Rikard Hedvall, RAÄ.

and antler were mixed with unworked animal bone in the bottom later, which was dated to the twelfth–thirteenth century. The layer covered ard marks in the untouched sand. Questions which remain to be answered are whether the deposits arose on the site or were transported there as fertilizer. The thickness of the deposits indicates settlement nearby. If the layers were deposited on the site, this would mean an extension of the previously assumed area of the central place.

The Dominican friary of St Olaf and crafts associated with it

The Dominican friary in Skänninge was built at the start of the thirteenth century and was completely destroyed by a fire at the end of the same century. At the start of the fourteenth century the friary was rebuilt. Remains of the friary have previously been investigated on several different occasions. The results have shown that the friary itself was on a marked rise in the present-day Munkgärdet (see fig. 4). Scholars have assumed

48

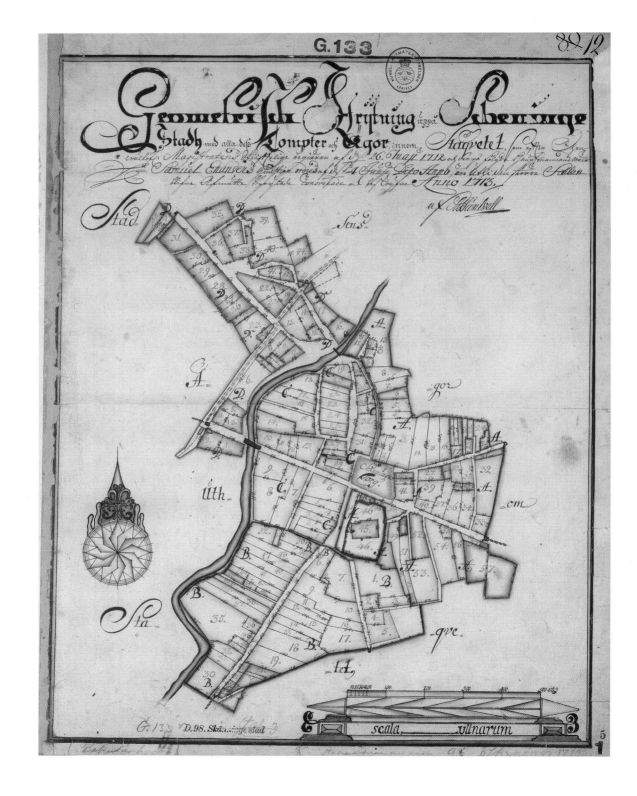

*Geometrisk Afrytning uppå Schenninge
Stadh med alla deß Tompter och Ägor innom Staqvetet ...*

Anno 1713.

scala ullnarum

that many of the outbuildings were south of the friary itself. Stone paving and remains of a forge have been excavated. The excavations in 1999 showed that the two phases of the friary are probably represented in the area. Both occupation layers and features in the form of walls, stone paving, and brick floors have been found. As for the outbuildings or workshops of the friary, there are still questions on the eve of the final excavation. The initial excavations showed that there were remains of features both north and south of the friary indicating relatively extensive workshop activities. The datings indicate that the features can be associated with the earliest phase of the establishment of the friary and are also contemporaneous with the workshop activities west of the river.

The remains of a bronze foundry were discovered only about 50 m north-west of the friary. Can the activities be linked to it? If so, perhaps they belong to the construction of the monastery, for example, when the church bells were cast. Radiocarbon analysis dates the feature to *c.* 1160 – 1280 AD. Few bronze-casting sites have been investigated in Scandinavia, and the sites that have been found in Sweden are often associated with bell-casting sites (Ahnund 1999). Nothing like this has previously been found beside a monastery, however. A little further north were traces of workshop activities in the form of presumed remains of forge hearths. A ^{14}C sample from these gave a date of 1190 – 1290 AD. There is a possibility that the activities are older than the Dominican friary, which was opened in 1237. They could thus be contemporary with the workshop activities west of the river. Together they would in this case constitute a very large craft area from the time before the town was founded.

In the area south of the monastery there may also have been some form of metalwork. Features investigated here at the end of the 1950s were interpreted as

a forge belonging to the friary. More features and sooty layers have been found by the ongoing investigations. These likewise probably derive from some type of workshop activity. Finds of iron slag indicate smithing.

South of the monastery area, ditches were also found. These follow the course of the town's eastern boundary as marked in the map of 1713 (fig. 7). Is this also the medieval boundary of the town? How was this boundary marked, apart from the ditches? To the far south was some stone paving which was probably the surface of one of the roads leading to the town, the medieval Linköpingsgatan. Did this come about in connection with the founding of the monastery, or when the main square, Stora Torget, was established in the town centre? The construction of the street must have led to a major restructuring of the town plan.

Conclusion

On the basis of the formerly known sources about Skänninge as a central place before it became a town in the formal sense, it was assumed that settlement was relatively limited and to begin with partly of a seasonal character. The early remains were confined to an area west of the river by St Martin's church, the crossing of the river at Järntorget, and a larger area, the actual plateau, south of All Saints' church. On the basis of this limited archaeological evidence, it was concluded that there was a market place on the east side of the River Skenaån, between the two churches. South of the market place was one of the two early medieval churches, All Saints'. Scholars have interpreted this church as belonging to a royal estate connected with the village of Biskopsberga north of the town. Beside and south of the church, a limited amount of very fragmentary archaeological material has been found, but sufficient to indicate that there was settlement in the area in the oldest phase of the history of the church in the eleventh century. On the other side of the river, at the other early medieval church, St Martin's, which presumably stood on the same site as the convent, excavations have shown that there was contemporary settlement beside the church, which has

Fig. 7. The oldest map of Skänninge is from 1713. The map shows surveys of plots and land as measured by the surveyor Matias Sundvall. Excavations revealed ditches which agreed with the field boundaries in the east. The map is in the Central Office of the National Land Survey in Gävle.

been interpreted as showing that the church belonged to a magnate's farm on the same site.

An ongoing archaeological project in connection with the expansion of the railway on the eastern edge of the town started in 1999 – 2000. The preliminary findings of the project include remains which cast fascinating new light on the early history of Skänninge. The results also hint that our picture of the oldest history of the place will partly change. The excavation area is on the eastern edge of medieval Skänninge, covering a total stretch of just over 1 km outside the area of the town as shown on the oldest map.

The conclusions that can be drawn from the preliminary results are that large areas outside the town centre have remains from the Late Iron Age or Early Middle Ages, the time when Skänninge as a central place probably emerged. The extent of the central place may thus be much larger than has hitherto been assumed. The coming excavations may thereby supplement the hitherto prevailing picture of the central place of Skänninge, for which the only source material used to be the large number of runestones, two early churches, and a few small-scale excavations. The planned project will give good opportunities to illuminate the history of Skänninge on several different levels. One of the main aims of the excavations in the town is to shed light on the development, extent, character, and function of Skänninge as a central place in the Late Iron Age and Early Middle Ages (cf. Lindeblad 2000; Nielsen 2000).

Some questions that may receive answers from the continued investigations in Skänninge are: What different crafts are represented, and on what scale were they pursued? How were crafts organized? Another interesting question is how settlement was structured and when it was established. In an earlier work Margareta Hasselmo has pointed out an area close to St Martin's church as the possible site of a magnate's farm. Written sources show that the church in the second half of the thirteenth century belonged to a magnate's family (Hasselmo 1987, p. 251). Some of the material presented above could possibly have been part of this property.

Other questions to which we are seeking answers are whether the settlement was regulated, what type of settlement it was, whether it was permanent or seasonal, and what type of activities besides crafts occurred. These important questions concern not only Skänninge, since they are common to many central places in Sweden. The excavation of the early medieval deposits will also elucidate the restructuring of settlement that may have taken place when the two monasteries were founded. The change may be able to tell us when the founding of the city began.

The development of Skänninge from a central place to a town can also be put in a larger spatial context allowing the discussion of the mutual relationship of early towns and central places. A place like Skänninge is considered to be one in a series of several central places included in a system in the Early Middle Ages which grew up as a result of an increasingly strong royal power (Hasselmo 1992, p. 50). Skänninge can also be compared with another medieval town in Östergötland, Söderköping, which is to be presented in a forthcoming doctoral dissertation (Broberg and Hasselmo, in prep.). The results will give opportunities for interesting comparisons between these two towns which show a partly similar pattern in the Early Middle Ages. Both Söderköping and Skänninge can be defined as early medieval central places with a church on either side of a river flowing through the town. In Söderköping the archaeological findings have shown that, to begin with, c. 1000–1150, the place was seasonally used as a reloading/market place. In the period c. 1150 – 1200 there was sparse settlement, with hints of regulation, and in the thirteenth century the town grew to its full extent (Tesch 1987, pp. 293 ff.). Did the development of Skänninge follow a similar pattern? Or does the seemingly large settlement as early as the eleventh and twelfth centuries represent a different course of evolution for the place? As we have seen, there are many questions to which answers will be sought in the final excavation of the central place on the eastern edge of Skänninge.

■ **Ann-Lili Nielsen**

References

Ahnund, J. 1999. *Gjutanläggning för kyrkklocka i Vendel. Arkeologiska undersökningar 1994 – 96.* Arkeologiska forskningslaboratoriet. Stockholm

Cnattingius, B., and Lindahl, A. 1970. Skänningetraktens fornminnen. In Lindahl, A. (ed.), *Skänninge stads historia.* Linköping.

Ersgård, L. 2000. Östergötland under medeltid och början av nyare tid – en arkeologisk översikt. In *Vetenskaplig verksamhetsplan för UV Öst. Arkeologiskt program 2000 – 2002.* Rapport UV Öst 2000:21. Linköping.

Hasselmo, M. 1983. *Skänninge.* Riksantikvarieämbetets och Statens historiska museer rapport: Medeltidsstaden 40. Stockholm.

Hasselmo, M. 1987. Skänninge. In Andrae, T., Hasselmo, M., and Lamm. K. (eds.), *7000 år på 20 år. Arkeologiska undersökningar i Mellansverige.* RAÄ. Stockholm.

Hasselmo, M. 1992. From Early-Medieval Central-Places to High-Medieval Towns – Urbanization in Sweden from the End of the 10th Century to c. 1200. In Ersgård, L., Holmström, M., and Lamm, K. (eds.), *Rescue and Research. Reflections of Society in Sweden 700 – 1700 A.D.* RAÄ, Arkeologiska undersökningar, Skrifter 2. Stockholm.

Lindeblad, K. 2000. Urbaniseringen i Östergötland. In *Vetenskaplig verksamhetsplan för UV Öst. Arkeologiskt program 2000 – 2002.* Rapport UV Öst 2000:21. Linköping.

Lindeblad, K., and Nielsen, A.-L. 2000. Centralplatser i västra Östergötland 200 – 1200 e Kr. Ett första försök till rumslig analys. In Nicklasson, P. (ed.), *Visingsöartiklar. Tolv artiklar om Visingsö från bronsålder till medeltid.* Jönköpings läns museum, rapport 42. Jönköping.

Lindqvist, G. 1970. Allhelgonakyrkan i Skänninge. In Lindahl, A. (ed.), *Skänninge stads historia.* Linköping.

Lovén, C. 1996. *Borgar och befästningar i det medeltida Sverige.* Stockholm.

Neill, T., and Lundberg, S. 1994. Förnyad diskussion om "Eskilstunakistorna". *Fornvännen* 89.

Nielsen, A.-L. 2000. Centrala platser i Östergötland under järnålder. In *Vetenskaplig verksamhetsplan för UV Öst. Arkeologiskt program 2000 – 2002.* Rapport UV Öst 2000:21. Linköping

Olsson, I., Stahre, N.-G., and Ståhle, C. I. 1969. *Rannsakningar efter antikviteter* II. Stockholm.

Roslund, M. 2001. *Gäster i huset. Kulturell överföring mellan slaver och skandinaver 900 – 1300.* Lund.

Tesch, S. 1987. Söderköping. In Andrae, T., Hasselmo, M., and Lamm. K. (eds.), *7000 år på 20 år. Arkeologiska undersökningar i Mellansverige.* RAÄ. Stockholm.

Investigation reports from ongoing projects in Skänninge, not mentioned in the text

Carlsson, T. *et al.* 2000. *Ett arkeologiskt linjeprojekt i västra Östergötland. Arkeologiska utredningar etapp 2 och förundersökningar.* RAÄ rapport, UV Öst 2000:12. Linköping.

Hedvall, R. 2000. *Arkeologisk förundersökning område 13 och 17 Skänninge.* RAÄ rapport, UV Öst. Linköping.

Introduction

The city of Norrköping was long typified by its role as one of the leading industrial centres of Sweden. Today, however, the workers' town is being reshaped into a lively university city and cultural centre. A beautiful, characteristic industrial setting by the last falls in the River Motala (Motala Ström) is being preserved with a new content, as old factory buildings are converted into exhibition halls and lecture theatres (fig. 2). From an archaeological perspective the transformation, which calls for extensive digging for pipelines and cables and the construction of new buildings in the city centre, means that surviving parts of older occupation layers are disappearing rapidly in a city that was already subject to extensive development. The growing pace of development also highlighted gaps in our archaeological knowledge of the city, and the need for a problem-oriented approach to excavations became obvious.

The city of Norrköping

Norrköping is situated at a central point in the landscape, bearing the stamp of two topographical elements, the river and a ridge to the south of it. The water route from Vättern, the large lake that divides southern Sweden into the two provinces of Västergötland and Östergötland, flows into the Baltic Sea here. Via a lake system, the River Motala links Vättern to the Baltic, and where it flows into the Bråviken bay it forms several mighty waterfalls as the water makes its way between small islands. The falls and the obstacles in the river at Norrköping were ideal for permanent fisheries and powering mills. In the sixteenth century, when the Renaissance prince Gustav Vasa ruled the country and the written sources became more ample, there were no fewer than twenty mills in the town. Water power was later crucial for the development of the place into an early industrial centre, and the area on the banks of the river has been used intensively until the present day.

Spatial organization

Norrköping's street grid was gradually regulated, receiving its modern appearance after a couple of fires in 1655 and 1719. Maps of the town from the seventeenth and eighteenth centuries show the spatial transformation of the town from an older irregular system of streets and different-shaped blocks to the strictly regulated modern town plan (figs. 3 and 4). The oldest map of the town was drawn up in 1640 in connection with the creation of a rectangular town plan. The map was drawn as a plan of the existing street grid, the central parts of which probably went back to a medieval town plan. It gives an idea of the extent of the town and its overall structure in the first half of the seventeenth century, before the regulation of the town. It shows streets and blocks, but the configuration of the blocks is not explained. We do not know what forces governed the design or how far back it goes. Nor are the seventeenth-century plot boundaries or buildings marked. The map shows a structural difference within the urban area. The blocks along the river

Fig. 1. The seal of Norrköping depicts St Olaf sitting on his throne with his crown, orb, and sceptre. It is mentioned for the first time in 1363. The illustrated seal comes from 1384. Photo: National Archives.

Fig. 2. Large factories along the River Motala dominate the inner city of Norrköping. Water power from the falls in the river have been used for a long time, and the area around the river has undergone great changes. Photo: Jan Norrman, RAÄ.

were small and criss-crossed by many alleys. A little distance away from the water, the blocks were bigger. The map seems to reflect a phase when small-scale, dense urban settlement was located beside the river and larger townyards were more dispersed at a certain distance from the water. The medieval town centre is assumed to have been on the ridge, where the two churches stand, but an administrative centre near these need not mean that settlement was denser there. The buildings in the town may have been spread over a larger area at an early stage, which partly explains the absence of thick layers and the difficulty of identifying medieval remains. Perhaps we should rather look for slightly denser settlement along the banks of the river, where the economically significant fishing and milling were located, and where the map shows the small blocks.

The point of departure

The current transformation of Norrköping is not just a modern phenomenon. In a well-established place, processes of change as society develops are a historical reality. Then, as now, symbols and fixed points are preserved, but the course of events is delineated archaeologically as the material content and social connotations change. General alterations to the spatial organization of the place can be detected in the formation of occupation layers, reflecting thoroughgoing changes in the history of the place. In the heavily developed industrial city of Norrköping, however, medieval layers have only been identified in a few places, and the earlier spatial organization of the town is an archaeological problem. Norrköping's occupation layers are difficult to analyse and interpret. They are as a rule sandy and

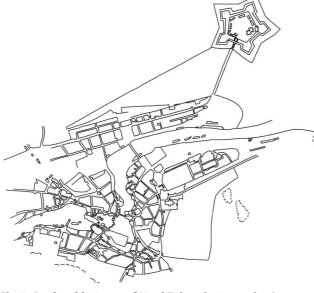

Fig. 3. On the oldest map of Norrköping, the town plan is made up of a network of streets and blocks of different sizes and shapes. The map was drawn up in 1640 by Olof Hansson Örnhuvud as a plan of the existing town in preparation for a projected regulation of the town. Graphics: Lars Östlin, RAÄ.

heavily compacted, and organic material is poorly preserved. A great deal of earth has been dug up and moved in the past. Trenches for pipelines have been legion, in contrast to excavations covering larger areas. As a consequence, the results of archaeological investigations are often difficult to put into a meaningful context. This situation makes it urgent to focus on analyses of early overall spatial structures and organization. A study of the distribution and character of the early remains, linked to key phases in the history of the place, will be used here as an analytical method in which the early history of Norrköping is sketched in three main phases.

Central place – medieval town – early modern town

In Norrköping we first glimpse a phase in the Early Middle Ages when it was a central place before it became a town proper in the fourteenth century, but it was not until the seventeenth century that the town expanded to become Sweden's leading industrial centre. The predecessor of the town has been characterized

as a village combining farming with fishing and milling, but the location and extent of the village site are unknown. In the Late Middle Ages the town consisted of four neighbourhoods, attested in written sources, but our knowledge of the structure and character of the town is limited. Sweden's Age of Greatness in the seventeenth century meant a vigorous expansion, but for this phase too there are serious gaps in our knowledge, since it has been relegated to the background in attempts to detect medieval remains. The oldest town centre from the time before the regulation gives us a picture of the town that is in many ways unexplained.

The central place – the early medieval fishing and milling village

In the Early Middle Ages the name of Norrköping is associated with an agrarian village with fishing and milling, when a degree of market trade was probably carried on (Ljung 1965). There is a great deal to suggest that this village was also a central place with overarching functions under royal influence. The initiative to build two churches on the crest of the ridge south of the river was a manifestation of the Early Middle Ages, preceding the time when Norrköping can begin to be regarded as a town. The two churches, together with the mills and the permanent fisheries, signal that Norrköping even in the Early Middle Ages had a different status from that of an ordinary peasant village.

Village

Norrköping in the Early Middle Ages, despite its special position, can in one respect be viewed as a farming village. The land owned by the village can be detected in a number of town lands which later retained the old division into *attung* units, a common principle of division in the villages of the Östergötland plain, originally meaning an "eighth" (Ljung 1965, p. 49). One of the two churches, dedicated to St John, was the parish church. Together with its cemetery, it constituted the centre of a parish with the same name as the village. Parish formation in the area goes back

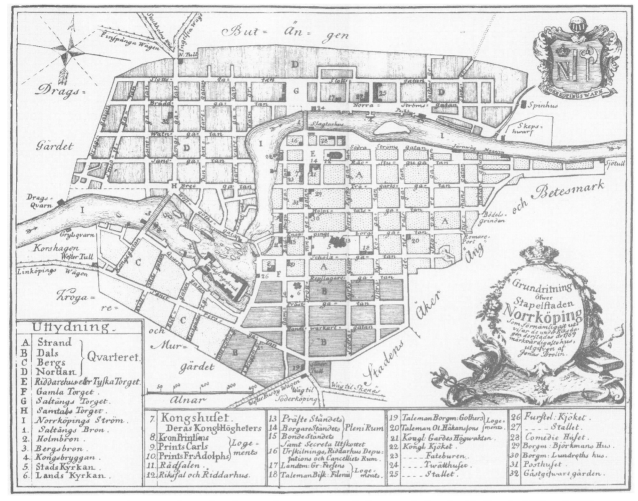

Fig. 4. Norrköping's modern, strictly regulated town plan was successively created after the big fires in 1655 and 1719. In preparation for the Diet of Norrköping in 1769, this ground plan of the town was published. It shows the most noteworthy buildings for the benefit of members of the diet and other visitors. As a predecessor of modern-day tourist maps it gives a good idea of the bygone town. The districts of Strand A, Dal B, Berg C, and Nordantill D are shown, as are the town church 5, the rural parish church 6, and the square F. Between Berg and Nordantill one can see the large Kvarnholmen and several other islets. Map from *Stadsingenjörskontorets jubileumsportfölj* 1984.

to the Early Middle Ages, when other parish churches around Norrköping were erected. The fact that St John's church was built as a Romanesque stone church is also suggested by early depictions and by foundation walls under a later church building (Broberg 1984, p. 55). The long history of Norrköping before the formation of the town is virtually unknown. By analogy with excavated villages in Östergötland, including some in the Norrköping area, we may assume that the establishment of settlement in a permanent location on a village site took place in the Late Iron Age or Early Middle Ages (Lindgren-Hertz 1997a). The village site was probably close to the parish church, but the location has not been identified. The site of rural medieval villages is otherwise usually possible to identify on early maps. Geometrical surveys are of good assistance for localizing village sites and determining the physical appearance of villages. At the time when the early land survey maps were drawn up, however, Norrköping had grown to become the town surveyed on the oldest map from 1640, when the village site can no longer be traced.

Trading place

Norrköping's role as a trading place at the transition between the Late Iron Age and the Middle Ages is evidenced in the place-name element -köpinge. Redirection of trade to new places has been noticed in many parts of Scandinavia. Norrköping's trading function may have been taken over from an older market place at Herrebro, further inland, where production was abandoned in the eleventh century (Lindeblad 1997).

Power

Apart from farming and trading, fishing and milling by the waterfalls in the river were important sources of livelihood in the village, as they were later in the town. The milling fee was a way for those in power to acquire part of the peasants' surplus, and the initiative to build and run corn mills lay with the king and the temporal and spiritual nobility from the start of the Middle Ages. The first mention of Norrköping in writing, in connection with a donation in 1283, reflects the interest of the king and the authorities in the village, and also the importance of the fishery. The donation concerns a salmon fishery in Norrköping which was given to the convent in Skänninge by Queen Sofia. We also have a hint of the crown's early interest in the village in the capacity of landowner and church builder. The second church in the village, dedicated to St Olaf, was built on crown land in Norrköping. When the church is later referred to as the town church in written sources, the right of patronage has been transferred to the Cistercian abbey in Askeby, but St Olaf's parish in Norrköping continued to be a regal pastorate and as such was originally crown property. A castle

started by King Birger Magnusson c. 1300, but never finished, may have been built on land belonging to the crown or the king in Norrköping (Ljung 1965, p. 11). This record is sometimes assumed to refer to the castle of Ringstadholm west of the town. A seventeenth-century tradition, however, puts a castle in the highly strategic position beside the oldest bridge in Norrköping, below the last waterfall, where large amounts of old masonry have been found since the eighteenth century (Lovén 1996, p. 111).

Centrality

The early strategic importance of Norrköping is highlighted by the place-name Ledungshammar, just east of the town, referring to an assembly point for the naval organization (ledung). The context as a whole with two churches, one of them a parish centre, the other a regal patron church, perhaps a castle, and economically significant mills and fisheries, makes it likely that a royal point of support was located in Norrköping. A hint that there may have been a royal manor in the village in the Early Middle Ages comes from a place-name analysis. Alos- or Alusagärdhe was the name of one of the town's most attractive fields (gärde). The element -hus "house", probably in the sense of a royal house, is compounded here with a first element of less certain meaning, either al- "cult centre" or adhal- "main/chief". Etymologically, Adhalhus could be the name of a manor in a complex of crown properties in and around Norrköping (Moberg 1965, p. 67). A complex like this in the Late Iron Age and Early Middle Ages may be compared with the system of collaborating farms with different central functions that is detected by archaeological investigations around Norrköping (Lindeblad 1997). We can also understand the patron church of St Olaf on royal land as part of an estate formation connected to the manor of Adalhus. The location of St Olaf's church is somewhat peripheral in relation to the town centre around the square. It has been thought that this site was chosen because the church was built so late that more central land was already occupied (Broberg 1984, p. 62). Another explanation for the location is that the church was built beside a manor. At the time when the town was founded, the right of patronage of St Olaf's church had been transferred to Askeby abbey through a royal donation. The economic framework of the estate complex may have consisted of parts of the abbey's other assets in the town, such as fisheries, mills, plots, fields, and islands, which may have been part of the donation. Royal economic interests in milling and fisheries can also be seen in name forms with *konung* "king", such as Konungskvarnen, Konungskaret, Konungsvarpet, and Konungslanen, which are common in Norrköping.

The medieval town
- the little town by the big fisheries
The description of Norrköping in the heading is taken from the history of the city, *Norrköpings historia*, which deals, among other things, with the question of the age of the town. An evaluation of the assembled documentary evidence suggests that the town can scarcely be taken back further than the first half of the fourteenth century, thereby refuting an earlier tradition claiming that the town was founded in the twelfth century (fig. 1). After the founding of the town, the documents indicate that Norrköping remained a small place throughout the Middle Ages, and it was not until the early modern period that it expanded to become one of the most important cities in Sweden (Ljung 1965).

The urban area
The urban area has been reconstructed on the basis of details in a document from 1384 in which the boundaries of the town are established by King Albreckt (Ljung 1965, p. 44). The late medieval town consisted of four districts attested in writing: Strand, Dal, Berg, and Nordantill. The town centre is assumed to have been located on the ridge south of the river. Beside the topographically suitable nature of this location, the assumption is based on the fact that the two medieval churches, the rural parish church of St John and the town church of St Olaf, were built on the crest of the ridge. The town square was also in the centre, which was made up of the districts of Strand and Dal. The only known medieval bridge was below the last waterfall. The bridge led to the district of Nordantill, north of the river, where the main road to Bergslagen and central Sweden followed a joint course, parallel to the river, before it split in two different directions. The road to the Östergötland plain and the episcopal city of Linköping proceeded from the centre of the town, running west via the Berg district, south of the river. Roads led southwards to other important points in the surrounding medieval landscape (fig. 5).

A description of the archaeological situation in Norrköping was published in 1984 in *Norrköping*, report no. 50 from the "The Medieval Town" project (Broberg 1984), when there had been little archaeological activity. The localization of urban settlement was a problem then, since medieval buildings had never been found in the medieval town centre. As a whole, medieval remains have only been identified in a few places in the town. With one exception, these are outside the town centre; they tend to be close to the river instead.

The northern part of the town
Three medieval ecclesiastical institutions are attested in written sources in Norrköping; besides the churches there is a mention of a chapel of St Gertrude on one occasion in 1543, when the crown owned four plots "north of the bridge at Saint Gertrude's chapel". Unlike the churches, the chapel was thus not in the town centre but in the Nordantill district. St Gertrude's chapel has not been found, but it must have been beside the north road leading out of the town. Settlement was established in Nordantill in the Late Middle Ages, and parts of the street grid were laid out. The medieval remains consist of buildings from the late fourteenth or early fifteenth century and of a burial place which probably belonged to St Gertrude's chapel, added in the fifteenth century (Svensson 1982). Another part of the medieval townscape was a log-paved alley leading down to the main road; new logs were laid on

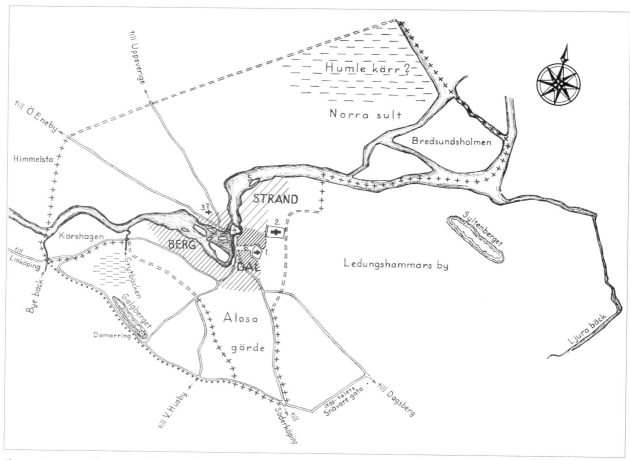

Fig. 5. Reconstruction map of the medieval urban area of Norrköping. From Ljung 1965.

several occasions. This particular alley was not regulated when the street grid was given its modern form; it still survives as one of the few reminders of the medieval town plan in Norrköping. The medieval remains were separated from the main road by a flow of water which probably originated in a natural spring but was reinforced and kept open with the aid of successively dug channels. The trench in which the water flowed, which was wide and deep, was a dominant feature in the early townscape. It demarcates the medieval burial ground from the secular part of the town with the mills and fisheries down by the river. It may also have been an important factor for the localization of St Gertrude's chapel. When it was filled in,

it meant a radical restructuring of the Nordantill district, which is probably connected with extensive construction work elsewhere in the town, perhaps at the time when Gustav Vasa owned plots in the area or else contemporary with early industrial construction down at the river. After being filled in, the burial place was claimed for buildings in the early modern period (Lindgren-Hertz 1998a,b).

The town centre

As in Nordantill, and establishment phase outside the town centre begins during the Middle Ages in the Berg district on the opposite, southern side of the river (Hållans *et al.* 1999; A.-C. Feldt, Östergötland County

Museum, pers. com.). In view of the crucial significance of the waterfalls for Norrköping, it is possible that the medieval evidence, with a distribution over a large area around the river, is to some extent a representative picture of the early spatial organization of the town. The dominance of the river must have meant that several central activities of the town were located on the riverbanks and the islands. The economically important mills and the localization of the permanent fisheries in the River Motala may have meant that large areas beside the river as well as many of the islands were also interesting for settlement. If so, the medieval town had a spatial extent that was not tied to the immediate vicinity of the two medieval churches. In the town centre on the ridge, around the two medieval churches, the excavated townyards were established in the sixteenth century at the earliest (Parr 1981; Kjellén 1996). Occasional finds of medieval pottery nevertheless indicate a medieval presence in the area, and the lack of buildings in the town centre is explained not only by the spread of the medieval town over a larger area. Based on the assumption that settlement must have been established earlier than the sixteenth century, it has been asked whether this really was the first settlement in the place or if evidence of previous settlement was dug away at an early stage (Broberg 1984, p. 53). This question arose again recently when medieval buildings were documented for the first time in the town centre. The thick, complex deposits here have no counterpart in Norrköping (Lindgren-Hertz 1999a). The interesting results of the excavation are discussed in the next article in this book.

The early modern town and the oldest town map

The early spatial organization of Norrköping is an archaeological problem in several respects. Medieval deposits are found in few places. Our knowledge of medieval Norrköping consequently has large gaps, but the archaeological knowledge of developments in the early modern period is also defective, since this period is given low priority in relation to the Middle Ages. In this case, however, there has been a swing, with townyards from the sixteenth and seventeenth centuries being excavated in order to provide answers to specific questions, as exemplified by an excavation in the Berg block, treated in the following article in this volume (see also Hållans *et al.* 1999). The archaeological evidence as a whole suggests a new era during the seventeenth century when Norrköping gradually expanded to become the country's leading industrial town. The period of the early town is overlain by heavily stratified layers of sand. Similar layers with fairly unmixed subsoil material are found at several places in Norrköping. They may be regarded as specially spread levelling layers, closing off one phase in the town and initiating a new one. Norrköping's levelling layers, however, are not associated with one single occasion in the history of the town; they rather seem to recur regularly in connection with various changes in settlement. Brick and lime mortar are introduced in the new phase to a much greater extent than before, when brick only occurred sporadically. Buildings and other traces of activities in the townyards also leave clearer traces, while the finds simultaneously become richer.

Spatial expansion

Medieval settlement has never been observed on the outer edge of the town, but in the early modern period it is possible to demonstrate the establishment of settlement on the edges of Berg and Nordantill as well, south and north of the river respectively, where sparsely built-up areas preceded the denser settlement structure from the eighteenth and nineteenth centuries. In the same way as with earlier changes of settlement, levelling layers of sand were spread here when the area was replanned according to a rectangular system in the eighteenth century.

South of the river, in the Berg district, the earlier topography was radically changed. A southern channel of the river with islets was eliminated with the aid of filling. The bank, on which several mill wheels are marked on the 1640 map, ran where there is now a street, and small alleys led down to the water. A section

Fig. 6. At several places in the Nordantill district, barrel-vaulted brick cellars were built in the early modern period. The one in the picture was built on the former burial ground of St Gertrude's chapel, a location which clearly shows the changed character of the area. Photo: Håkan Ahldén.

of the boundary laid out by King Albreckt in 1384 was located here, as was the exit from the town towards Linköping via Grytbäcken (Ljung 1965, p. 44; cf. fig. 5). Excavations in the area have mainly uncovered buildings from the eighteenth and nineteenth centuries (Syse 1986; Flodin 1990). The earliest layer in the place is a cultivation layer formed by the townspeople's agriculture within the town ramparts. Layers of a similar character have been found at several paces within the urban area. They may be assumed to represent cultivation that had gone on since prehistoric times, continuing when the town was founded, and stopping at different points depending on how fast the town expanded. The cultivation in the area has recently been shown to be overlain by seventeenth-century remains, which dates the establishment of settlement on the edge of the town south of the river to the Age of Greatness.

North of the river, in the district of Nordantill, barrel-vaulted brick cellars were built at this time (fig.

6). A cellar built on the former burial ground of St Gertrude's chapel clearly shows the changed character of the area. The building was retracted a little way from the street in the present-day block. It was oriented to the predecessor of the current street, which is depicted on the earliest town map as being inexplicably asymmetrical at this section. In the outer area north of the river the present-day square was likewise an open place on the earliest map. Streets radiated from it towards the town centre and out towards the exit roads. On the outer edge, beyond the square, a survey of buildings in the 1940s revealed the coming of the new era, in the form of a rectilinear town plan. The oldest buildings were constructed around 1750, oriented according to the present street grid. Archaeologically investigated buildings, including a barrel-vaulted brick cellar are oriented obliquely in relation to the current shape of the block, and the street layout shows that it belonged to an earlier block structure. The structures on the oldest maps were thus crucial for the analysis of the relation of the building to the overall form of the town. The map showed the present-day regular block spread out over five earlier irregular blocks, one big one right on the edge of the town and four smaller ones. In the earliest phase the whole area was used for cultivation within the town boundaries. Beginning around 1600, the area slowly changed character, as cultivation plots were gradually built on. Closest to the town, where the map shows small blocks, settlement quickly became dense, but where the map shows a bigger block on the edge of the town, settlement was not properly established until around 1800 (Lindgren-Hertz and Nielsen 1997; Lindgren-Hertz 1997b, 1998a,b, 1999b).

Fig. 7. Our oldest land survey maps do not have the same exactitude as modern maps. The incorrect measurements become obvious when modern maps are superimposed on early geometrical maps. To obtain a clearer idea of where in the bygone townscape archaeological remains are located, the early maps of Norrköping have been rectified by Elisabeth Essen, RAÄ UV Mitt. The modern town map was combined with the rectified map by Lars Östlin, RAÄ.

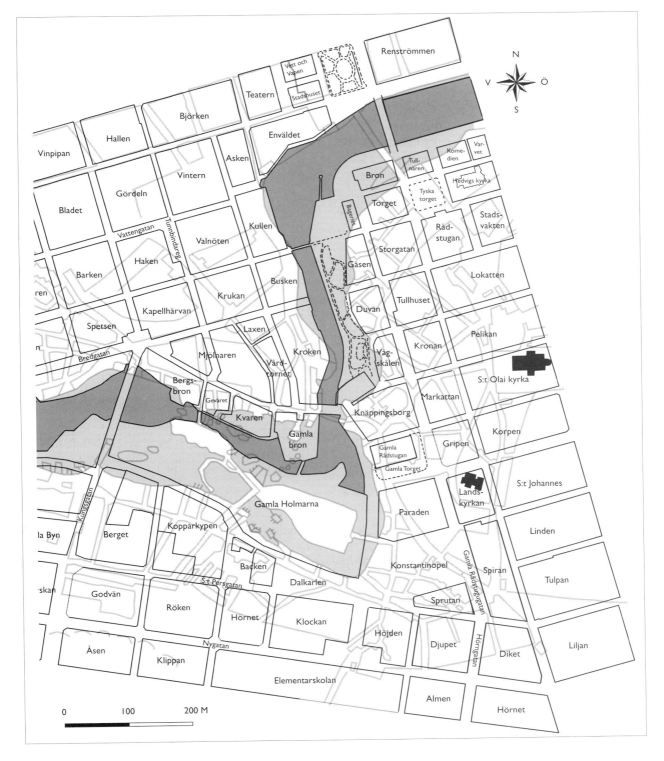

Renströmmen

Vett och Vapen
Teatern
Stadshuset
Björken
Hallen
Envaldet
Vinpipan
Asken
Komedien
Varvet
Tullnären
Vintern
Bron
Hedvigs kyrka
Gördeln
Bladet
Tyska torget
Torget
Stadsvakten
Kullen
Baseriet
Rådstugan
Valnöten
Storgatan
Vattengatan
Haken
Gåsen
Lokatten
Barken
Busken
Krukan
Tullhuset
Kapellhärvan
Duvan
Spetsen
Laxen
Kronan
Pelikan
Kroken
Mjölnaren
Vågskålen
Bredgatan
Värdtornet
S:t Olai kyrka
Bergsbron
Markattan
Geväret
Kvaren
Knäppingsborg
Korpen
Gamla bron
Gamla Rådstugan
Gripen
Gamla Torget
S:t Johannes
Gamla Holmarna
Landskyrkan
Linden
Kopparkypen
Paraden
Berget
la Byn
Konstantinopel
Spiran
Backen
S:t Persgatan
Dalkarlen
Sprutan
Tulpan
Godvän
Röken
Hörnet
Klockan
Höjden
Djupet
Diket
Liljan
Åsen
Nygatan
Klippan
Elementarskolan
Almen
Hörnet

0   100   200 M

The town map

The oldest map of Norrköping has been compared with the modern map on several occasions by overlay. Overlay maps give a good general idea of the relationship between different phases in the history of a town. Only rough agreement can be expected, however, which means uncertainty about the placing of old streets and blocks in the modern townscape. The overlay maps of Norrköping show largely the same overall picture of the town in 1640 and today, but the differences are considerable when one comes down to the level of the blocks. Since different overlays have been used alternately, this has consequences for the explanation of the early remains of the town. When analysing the overall spatial structures and organization of the town, it is essential to know where on the early maps the archaeological remains were found. This is particularly important in attempts to explain the shape of blocks and the courses of streets on the basis of the archaeological evidence. The placing of excavated buildings, for example, the stone houses, within the blocks is of great value for explaining the shape of the blocks, and consistent recurrent placing of the stone houses in the older block configurations should have a direct functional correlation. As a way to build up knowledge of the early spatial organization of Norrköping, the oldest town map, together with a number of early maps of the town and its surroundings, have been rectified (fig. 7). The rectification was an attempt to test the method used for historical overlay maps of rural villages to see whether it can be applied to early town maps. The former physical shape of the countryside, as shown in geometrical surveys, is rectified when traced against the modern economic map. The town map proved harder to work with, since it is at a different level of detail; moreover, Norrköping was complicated because the large-scale changes undergone by the town since the seventeenth century mean that there are few rectification points. The detailed work has scarcely begun, but spot checks show good agreement between archaeologically documented cellars and streets on the one hand and the appearance of blocks and streets on the traced maps. In comparative analyses of archaeological material and early maps, however, it is essential not to let the map govern the analysis; differences in source value must be considered. The map represents the overall spatial structure of the town at a frozen moment in time. Archaeology reflects a process and tries to capture events with a wide chronological span, from different segments of the town, within the framework of the overall structure.

Conclusion

In this article I have used three key periods with the aim of discussing the early spatial organization of Norrköping. In the Early Middle Ages we glimpse a phase as a central place when Norrköping, with two churches, permanent fisheries, and milling, was probably under the influence of the crown. The formation of the town, according to written criteria, took place in the Late Middle Ages, and urbanization was weak. In the early modern period the town expanded vigorously, developing into one of Sweden's leading industrial cities. The point of departure has been the many, often small-scale excavations, which made it important to focus on overall analyses if they were to make a meaningful contribution to the advancement of our knowledge of the town.

The spatial organization of medieval Norrköping has long been elusive. There are few medieval remains, mainly found close to the river outside the centre of the town proper. There may be several reasons for this state of affairs. One is the dramatic topography of the place, with large differences in level. Early removal of earth in connection with the restructuring of settlement appears to have been significant. Thick levelling layers preceded new building at several places in the town, and the large-scale milling at the falls in the river changed the waterside area a long time ago. An administrative centre where the two churches stand need not have meant that the area there was densely built up. The archaeologically documented medieval remains, with a spread over a large area outside the centre, may to a certain extent be a representative picture of the early spatial organization of Norrköping. The town, and perhaps also its predecessor the central place, may have been multicentre structures with settlement spread over a large area. The localization of the economically significant mills and fisheries on the river may have meant that large sections of the banks and many of the islets were attractive for settlement as well. In particular, the dominance of the river means that several central activities were placed outside the town centre. The material remains of medieval Norrköping may therefore be expected to have a wide spread, which means that the accumulated layers need not always be thick, and they could represent several activities, besides dwellings, which may be difficult to identify.

In the Age of Greatness the earliest town map, from 1640, gives a picture of the town's overall spatial structure with many inexplicable details. The map is not an ideal plan which was supposed to be implemented, but was drawn up as a map of the existing town for a planned regulation. Unlike the medieval town, the physical design of which we know virtually nothing

about, the map gives us an idea of the courses of streets and the shapes of blocks in the early modern town. The content of the blocks, what governed the design, and how far back it goes, on the other hand, are unknown factors. Comparative analyses of archaeological material and the rectified map open possibilities for a greater understanding of the relation of the overall structures to the town's stock of buildings and the development of settlement. The long archaeological perspective also contains the potential for analyses of the dynamic changes in the spatial organization of Norrköping from the Middle Ages to the seventeenth century.

■ **Lena Lindgren-Hertz**

Note

This article is a revised and abridged version of an article previously published in 2001 in *Från stad till land: En medeltidsarkeologisk resa tillägnad Hans Andersson*, ed. Anders Andrén, Lars Ersgård, and J. Wienberg (Lund Studies in Medieval Archaeology 29, Stockholm).

References

Broberg, B. 1984. *Norrköping*. Riksantikvarieämbetets och Statens historiska museer rapport: Medeltidsstaden 50. Stockholm.

Flodin, L. 1990. *Östergötland, Norrköping, Kvarteret Gamla Byn 3, Fornlämning 96*. Rapport 1990.

Hållans, A.-M., Karlsson, P., and Tagesson, G. 1999. *Kvarteret Dalkarlen. Bebyggelse och industri i stormaktstidens Norrköping RAÄ 96*. Rapport UV Öst 1999:1.

Kjellén, U. 1996. *1500- och 1600-talslämningar i kvarteret Gripen*. UV Stockholm, Rapport 1996:61.

Lindeblad, K. 1997. The Town and the Three Farms. On the Organization of the Landscape in and around a Medieval Town. In Andersson, H., Carelli, P., and Ersgård, L. (eds.), *Visions of the Past. Trends and Traditions in Swedish Medieval Archaeology*. Lund Studies in Medieval Archaeology 19. RAÄ, Arkeologiska undersökningar, Skrifter 24. Stockholm.

Lindgren-Hertz, L. 1997. Farm and Landscape. Variations on a Theme in Östergötland. In Andersson, H., Carelli, P., and Ersgård, L. (eds.), *Visions of the Past. Trends and Traditions in Swedish Medieval Archaeology*. Lund Studies in Medieval Archaeology 19. RAÄ, Arkeologiska undersökningar, Skrifter 24. Stockholm.

Lindgren-Hertz, L. 1997b. *Bebyggelseutveckling i kv Mjölnarens västdel (fd kv Trehörningen)*. Rapport UV Linköping 1997:33.

Lindgren-Hertz, L. 1998a. *Gatuschakt i stadsdelarna Nordantill och Berg*. Rapport UV Linköping 1998:16.

Lindgren-Hertz, L. 1998b. *Spår av en äldre stadsbild i kv Mjölnaren*. Rapport UV Linköping 1998:26.

Lindgren-Hertz, L. 1999a. *Mellan Landsförsamlingens kyrka och Strömmen. Kv Konstantinopel*. Rapport UV Linköping 1999:4

Lindgren-Hertz, L. 1999b. *1600-tal och äldre bronsålder i stadens västra utkant*. Rapport UV Linköping 1999:7

Lindgren-Hertz, L., and Nielsen, A.-L. 1997. *Kv Täppan 22 och 23*. Rapport UV Linköping 1997:35.

Ljung, S. 1965. Norrköpings historia. Tiden intill 1568. In Helmfrid, B., and Kraft, S. (eds.), *Norrköpings historia 1*. Stockholm.

Lovén, C. 1996. *Borgar och befästningar i det medeltida Sverige*. Stockholm.

Moberg, L. 1965 Norrköpingstraktens ortnamn. In Helmfrid, B., and Kraft, S. (eds.), *Norrköpings historia 1*. Stockholm.

Parr, M. 1987. *Spår av det medeltida Norrköping i kvarteret Kronan*. Rapport UV 1987:10.

Svensson, K. 1982. *Provundersökning inom kv Mjölnaren m fl, Norrköping, Östergötland*. Rapport 1982.

Syse, B. 1986. *Kv Kopparkypen, Norrköping, Östergötland*. Rapport 1986.

Introduction

The early history of Norrköping has long been regarded as difficult to capture archaeologically. When "The Medieval Town" project published its report on Norrköping in 1984, it was noted in the preface that there was little archaeological material (Broberg 1984). Moreover, the extant written sources are scant. It is not until the sixteenth century that written data about the town become plentiful. Although Norrköping was urbanized in the mid-fourteenth century, it was weak as a town, with few institutions (Lindeblad 2000, p. 59). The role of the place in the Middle Ages has been explained by the historian S. Ljung in terms of the proximity to the neighbouring town of Söderköping, which in this period was one of the biggest towns in Sweden, with flourishing trade and several important institutions (Ljung 1965, p. 78). It was not until the expansion of Norrköping as an early industrial town in the second half of the sixteenth century that the relative strength of the two towns was reversed.

The archaeological observations that were made in Norrköping until the mid-1980s were relatively numerous, but they mainly consist of small details which are of limited use due to insufficient documentation. In the inner city of Norrköping there has been extensive earthmoving in historical and recent times, which further complicates the picture. The state of archaeological knowledge of the city's history was thus restricted for a long time, leaving mostly only written sources to rely on. As a consequence of increased development in the city centre in the last ten years, however, we have had an opportunity to begin a new discussion of the course of urbanization. By combining the results of the small-scale archaeological investiga-

tions conducted in recent years with historical sources and maps, Lena Lindgren-Hertz has formulated three chronological archaeological problem areas proceeding from the early spatial organization of Norrköping, *the central place, the medieval town*, and *the early modern town* (Lindgren-Hertz, this volume; Lindgren-Hertz 2001, pp. 277 ff.).

This article is a description of how the National Heritage Board Eastern Excavations Department, UV Öst, has worked with two large archaeological investigations in Norrköping, the Dalkarlen and Konstantinopel blocks. Considerable space will be devoted to a presentation of the methodology and the theoretical pre-understanding behind the excavations. In addition, a couple of articles about the theoretical foundation of the excavation method will be discussed and evaluated. The cooperation between archaeology and quaternary geology in the project on the Konstantinopel block will also be described. The results of the two investigations will also be briefly presented. For a presentation of the history of Norrköping we refer to Lindgren-Hertz, this volume.

The Dalkarlen block

In 1998 there was a major archaeological investigation in the Dalkarlen block. It covered an area of about 350 square metres with layers up to 1 metre thick, mainly deposited in the seventeenth century, Sweden's Age of Greatness. Several smaller excavations have previously touched on this period, but with the excavation of the Dalkarlen block it was possible for the first time to study seventeenth-century remains and pursue the archaeology of modern times on a large scale and with an explicit focus on specific problems in Norrköping.

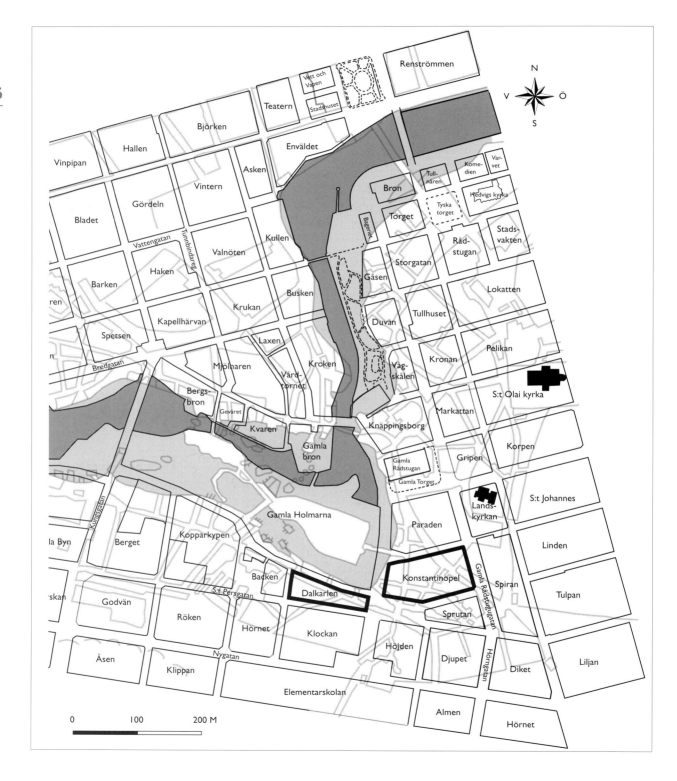

In the second half of the sixteenth century Norrköping underwent vigorous expansion in connection with the intensification of iron production in the mining area of Östergötland, which made the town important as an export harbour (Helmfrid 1965). Milling and fishing, which had been important economic activities in the Middle Ages, also increased at this time, besides which Norrköping acquired an important function in the administrative apparatus (Ersgård 2001, pp. 95 ff.). The first half of the seventeenth century also saw the foundation of a weapon factory, a brass works, and a glovery, which together constituted the foundation for the later development of Norrköping as one of the major industrial towns in Sweden (Helmfrid 1965; Broberg 1984). This early industry was called Holmens Bruk, which still survives as the name of a company today.

The Dalkarlen block is on the south bank of the River Motala in what was formerly called Bergskvarteret (see fig. 1). According to historical sources it was not until the second half of the sixteenth century and the start of the seventeenth century that the town of Norrköping expanded into this area. The excavations conducted in this part of the town basically support this thesis (Broberg 1984, pp. 34 ff.; Menander 2001). The population and the buildings on this side of the river have been interpreted as being attached to Holmens Bruk. The area was mainly inhabited by the German-speaking staff of the brass works, which is why it was also called Tyskebacken or "German Hill" (Helmfrid 1965, p. 295).

The area slopes sharply northward down to the river. According to the rectification of the 1640 map that was performed in connection with the investigation, the excavated site comprised parts of two large blocks. These were separated by an alley running east-west, and it is likely that the northern part of the site

was only a few metres south of the predecessor of the street Kvarngatan (Hållans *et al.* 1999; Karlsson in prep.). According to the same map, the excavated remains of settlement were about thirty metres south of the oldest attested south bank of the River Motala. Along this bank, in the immediate vicinity of the excavated area, the town historian Edvard Ringborg (1921) was able to identify the location of a copper hammer and a water-powered bark mill.

Before the excavation we formulated questions based on the state of archaeological knowledge about Norrköping. Although the written sources from the seventeenth century may be considered good, they do not give us any information about individual properties or households, nor about the character of the plots and the buildings, nor the form and function of the material culture. The role of archaeological source material for questions of this type is therefore very important. The main aims were thus to put the topographical and economic development of the town in a social and cultural context. The problems concerned the *establishment* of settlement in the area and hence the function and character of the place in different periods. There were also questions about the *spatial structure* as regards both the excavated blocks and the town as a whole. In addition, questions were formulated about *industrialization* and how it affected the social and mental structures in a residential block in the seventeenth century (Hållans *et al.* 1999).

Theory and method

For the excavation of the Dalkarlen block, a contextual method was used. The method originated in England, where it is called the "single context" method; it has been practised since the 1970s (Harris *et al.* 1993). A contextual method was chosen partly on the basis of the character of the remains and partly in order to answer the questions formulated by the project. The aim was to facilitate critical analyses of the archaeological record. It was thus crucial to interpret the creation of each stratigraphical unit in the field in order to assess its value as evidence (Tagesson 2000, p. 3).

Fig. 1. Plan of Norrköping combined with the oldest town plan from 1640. The Dalkarlen and Konstantinopel blocks are marked. It will be seen that the blocks are only 150 metres apart. The older course of the River Motala is marked in light grey, while today's course is shown in dark grey. Graphics: Lars Östlin, RAÄ.

Fig. 2. A cellar in the Vattnet block, Norrköping, excavated in winter 2001. Measuring about 12 by 7 metres, it has been dated to the 1620s – 40s (Karlsson *et al*. 2001). It was probably built on the same land as the estate of Norrköpingshus, which was built by King Gustav Vasa as a model farm. The dating of the cellar, however, rules out any link with the farm, which had burned down in 1604. The relatively large number of cellars excavated from this time in Norrköping could possibly be interpreted as a reflection of the good economy of the town in the expansion phase. Photo: Rikard Hedvall, RAÄ.

Documentation was done in the form of text and graphics. Both analogue and digital techniques were used for the graphic documentation. The system was based on the ambition of achieving something simple, stringent, and capable of subsequent processing with GIS (Geographic Information Systems) and a relational database in a network environment (Karlsson 2000, p. 35).

Working with a contextual method means, among other things, actively interpreting and trying to understand – while still in the field – the cultural conceptions behind the formation of the individual stratigraphical units, their spatial distribution, content, and in particular their preservation. The pre-understanding is that the occupation layers manifest culturally conditioned actions which may be of both conscious and unconscious character (Larsson and Johansson Hervén 1998; Larsson 2000, pp. 97 ff.). To ascertain the cultural-historical significance of the stratigraphical units and hence their value as evidence, a defined and explicit interpretative apparatus was applied to the Dalkarlen block with the aim of fitting the individual layers into a layer typology. This typology has its origin in the one worked out for the processing of the archaeological material from the excavation of the Sanden neighbourhood in Vadstena in 1995 – 96 (Hedvall *et al.* 2000, pp. 22 f.). The interpretative apparatus is intended to serve as a tool for the archaeologist in the field to make a cultural-historical interpretation of each stratigraphical unit and hence to assess its source value. The division of the layer typology is based on the manner of deposition, that is, whether the layer is a *primary*, *secondary*, or *tertiary* deposit, along with an assessment of the function of the layer. Primarily deposited layers are those containing material deposited where it was used, for example, a layer deposited on a floor. Secondary deposits consist of material which is contemporary with, but functionally and spatially separate from its original context of use; examples of secondarily deposited layers are waste layers. Tertiary deposits are layers which are functionally, spatially, and chronologically separate from their original context of use; examples of this are layers used for ground preparation. This means, for example, that the content of a primarily deposited layer, such as a floor layer, can be used for dating and identifying the function of a building (Tagesson 2000, p. 157).

Theoretically approaching layers with the aid of this interpretative apparatus means that one is partly forced to interpret the layers within a given framework. Some of the dynamic character of the material thus risks disappearing, but the advantages of interpreting the formation of the layers – and hence their source value – in the field outweighs this. The post-processing is made much easier, there are more approaches to the material, mass material becomes more manageable, and the cultural-historical interpretations rest on a firmer foundation.

On German Hill
- settlement development
in the Dalkarlen block

The results of the excavation in the Dalkarlen block have been divided into nine phases of settlement development. Each phase denotes a spatial and chronological context, and each new phase is the result of a demonstrable change in the character of the activities. The phases thereby reflect changed conditions for the use and physical form of the area.

The oldest remains were characterized by traces of late medieval activity which were difficult to interpret.

In the sixteenth century there was extensive ground preparation for the establishment of new settlement in the area; this involved marking out plots, which left traces in the form of ditches and fences along an alley. It was clear, however, that a fairly long time passed before the earliest settlement was actually established on the site.

The oldest settlement, which had an agrarian character with animal fences beside the houses, has been dated to the second half of the sixteenth century. There was then a development in the first half of the seventeenth century towards a more urban settlement with houses and yards. In the southern part of the site there was a forge at this time, dated to the 1630s. It contained temperable iron blanks and welding slag, which together indicate weapon manufacture. The weapon forge in the Dalkarlen block has been interpreted as being attached to the weapon factory in Holmens Bruk (Wallebom in prep.).

The buildings were finally destroyed by a fire which has been interpreted as the great fire of Norrköping in 1655. It was possible to trace an effort at rebuilding according to the old plot structure, but this was discontinued in favour of a regulated town plan, which in this part of the town was implemented in the 1660s. The great restructuring that this involved could be documented as extensive levelling layers, after which settlement was oriented according to the new town plan (Hållans *et al.* 1999).

Pottery, clay pipes, and waste management
- an evaluation

In accordance with the National Heritage Board's publication strategy, the results of the excavation of the Dalkarlen block have been reported in two stages. Immediately after the fieldwork was concluded, the findings were processed and compiled to provide access to the material. The report describes the circumstances of the excavation, the set goals, and the results of the excavation placed in their cultural-historical context.

The final publication has a broader and deeper analysis and interpretation of the material. It contains a total of eight articles which problematize in different

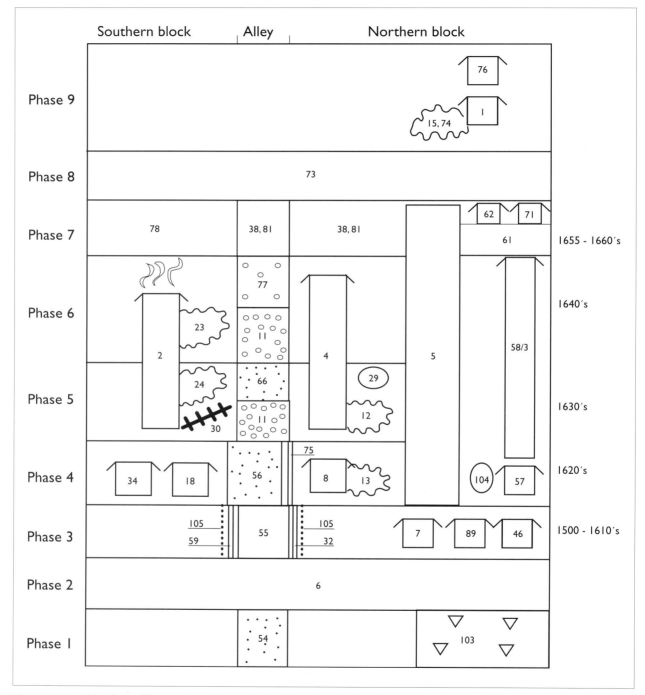

Fig. 3. A type of land-use diagram from the excavation of the Dalkarlen block and the chronological landmarks suggested on the basis of an analysis of the dates of clay pipes and coins (Hållans *et al.* 1999; Menander 2000, p. 150). Graphics: Lars Östlin, RAÄ.

ways the results of the excavation and shed light on the history of Norrköping. Two of the articles are about the formation of the layers and waste management, along with the possibility of dating the material with the aid of clay pipes. The articles proceed from the excavation method and are partly intended to evaluate the method and the interpretative apparatus. These two articles will be briefly summarized below.

In one article Göran Tagesson discusses and analyses the occupation layers and their content from the point of view of cultural history (Tagesson 2000, pp. 153 ff.). He discusses questions of artefact patterns and their representativeness. The basic premise is that a contextual excavation method is a useful tool for handling the source material, but in the article he assesses the layer typology that was formulated in advance. Tagesson asks how relevant and useful attempts to identify layer types are. By putting the find content of the layers in relation to the interpreted deposition type and hence the function, he evaluates the typology. In the article he studies the degree of fragmentation of the pottery in open and closed areas in order to show how the layers were used and affected. His study shows that, from a comparative analysis of sherd weights in the different layers, it is possible to test the cultural-historical interpretation of the layer. Tagesson concludes that bigger sherds, defined in the article as "not tread-friendly", mainly occur in secondary and tertiary deposits which were closed. In other words, sherds such as handles, shanks, and feet are chiefly represented in layers that were not trodden on, such as waste layers and filling layers. Finally, he discusses waste management on the basis of these circumstances. His conclusion is that the artefact patterns cannot be regarded as random; they are rather the result of deliberate selections, which are in turn culturally conditioned. Tagesson demonstrates in his analysis that the distribution of the finds in the layers is to a large extent linked to cultural conceptions about waste and its handling (Tagesson 2000, p. 170).

Yet another article proceeds from the contextual excavation method and the layer typology described above, but the aim here is to inquire into dating problems (Menander 2000, pp. 141 ff.). Hanna Menander investigates the possibility of using clay pipes for dating the stratigraphical sequence. The initial assumption is that the excavation method and the layer typology used for the excavation of the Dalkarlen block enable an evaluation of the source value of each layer. In addition, it is the question that dictates the choice of which layer and hence which finds can be used in the analysis. Since the article concentrates on the dating problem, it uses clay pipes and also coins from layers which are interpreted as having a high evidential value for dating, that is, from primary and secondary deposits. By comparing the dating of clay pipes and coins within one and the same contextual group and then relating the results to the stratigraphical sequence, several of the phases can be given chronological fixed points (see fig. 3). The author points out, however, that it is not possible to make a general selection based solely on given layer types or definitions. The selection was made after a careful critical reading of the description and interpretation of each individual layer. In addition, she claims that the most reliable dating results are obtained when one allows the datings of the artefacts to interact with the stratigraphical sequence and the historical sources (Menander 2000, p. 151). The result of the analysis shows that clay pipes can very well be used as a dating instrument. Moreover, the analysis confirms that the layer typology actually worked, with a few exceptions. The results thus corroborate the method, which means that the datings and the selection principles can also be applied to other material from the investigation. An ongoing project intended to date and build up chronological series for late red earthenware in Norrköping is partly based on this method and these results.

These two articles show how we have evaluated our approach and the excavation method on which the cultural-historical interpretations are based. The articles moreover shed light on the potential and focus on the benefits of combining the method with an explicit theoretical interpretative apparatus.

The Konstantinopel block

In autumn 1999 and summer 2000 parts of the Konstantinopel block were excavated. The total excavated area was about 350 square metres, with layers up to two metres thick. The excavation above all comprised high and late medieval remains, but there were also remains from the early modern period. This is the biggest and most comprehensive excavation in Norrköping from this period.

The Konstantinopel block is in Dal, the old part of the city between the rural parish church of St John and the River Motala (see fig. 1). The excavated site is in the area that has been pointed out as the centre of the medieval town, where importance has been attached to the proximity to the river, the old bridge, the old square, and the two medieval churches. The map from 1640 shows that the block spreads over several older streets and alleys, of which we have now found archaeological evidence with this excavation (Karlsson *et al.* in prep.). According to the same map, the roads to Söderköping, Linköping, and Västra Husby met south of the excavation site (Lindgren-Hertz 1999, pp. 5 ff.).

The excavated area lies on a spur of the slope of the Norrköping ridge, which means that the ground falls steeply towards the River Motala. According to the earliest map, a southern stream described a sharp bend just west of Konstantinopel and then continued northwards in and near the present Dalsgatan. The excavated area was much closer to the river than it is today, since the southern stream was filled in. Despite extensive removal and filling of earth ever since the Middle Ages, the differences in level between the eastern and western parts of the block are still considerable. A great difference in level also made itself felt in the excavation area. In the low-lying western part of the site the layers were very well preserved, whereas they were dried out and diffuse in the higher-lying eastern part.

The overall aim when the excavation started was to shed light on the urbanization process in Norrköping in terms of continuity and discontinuity, with the emphasis on the medieval development. Since there was virtually no archaeological source material from medieval Norrköping, it seemed important to answer fundamental questions about the *ground topography*, *dating*, and the *character of the place and the buildings*. Furthermore, we emphasized the importance of layer analyses for shedding light on changing activities in different periods and thereby capturing changes in the course of urbanization. Close collaboration was therefore established with a quaternary geologist (Jens Heimdahl). The aim was to determine the potential of macrofossil analysis of urban layers with a complicated stratigraphy. There was also a desire to interweave the results of the macrofossil analyses with the archaeological interpretations to a greater extent and thus contribute to the cultural-historical interpretations.

The material from the investigation has been processed in basically the same way as the material from the Dalkarlen block. One difference, however, is that the material from the Konstantinopel block is divided and presented in periods instead of phases. This may seem like a minor difference, but the definition of the different concepts has consequences for the continued interpretation. The periodization should be viewed as an attempt to capture overall courses and structures which can be understood and explained in a larger context than the individual excavation. The aim is that the results of the excavation will be easier to relate to hypotheses about the history of Norrköping based on other source material or future excavations in the city. In this way we have obtained results which can be put in relation to Lindgren-Hertz's three fixed points in chronology and cultural history: *the central place, the medieval town*, and *the early modern town*.

Archaeology and geology

From our experiences with the Dalkarlen project, we chose to investigate the Konstantinopel block with the same method and the same layer typology. The aim formulated for the project, however, required a more careful analysis of the content of the layers, and therefore great emphasis was attached to macrofossil analyses. To ascertain the potential of these analyses and to make the cooperation with the quaternary geologist succeed, he worked along with the archaeologists for most of the excavation, which proved to be fruitful. One of the difficulties of our collaboration and the attempt to work in a multidisciplinary way, however, was the linguistic barrier that exists between archaeologists and geologists. The terminology and concepts are the same or similar, but the meanings differ. The key words for the success of our collaboration were thus communication and discussion.

A subsidiary aim of the collaboration was to try to develop a working method for integrating the archaeological and the geological questions in the interpretations in the field. During the fieldwork, therefore, methods were developed to prepare and analyse macrofossil samples continuously in the layers that were being excavated. This method should be regarded as a preliminary analysis intended to give an idea of the rough composition of the sediment. Through the preliminary analysis, the information about the macrofossil content could be incorporated in the discussion and interpretation of the layer at the same time as it was being investigated.

The preliminary macrofossil analyses also helped to give a quick idea of how the layer was composed. Did the macrofossil content differ in different samples from the same layer, or was the layer homogeneous? What was the appearance of the biotope represented by the plant macrofossils? Were they meadow or wet meadow plants found in droppings of grazing animals, or were cultivated or collected plants mixed in the layer? Were there many root fibres or stem parts in the layer? Such information proved very useful during the discussion of layer composition, of whether an area was overgrown or not, and the function of constructions, in other words, information which can serve as a basis for the cultural-historical interpretation. In addition, the preliminary analysis was a foundation for further sampling for increased macrofossil analysis. Sampling could be optimized in this way, so that large volumes could be sampled in cases where macrofossils occurred sparsely. Sampling could also be concentrated in areas where specially interesting finds of fruits and seeds had been made.

Fig. 4. One of the thorn-apples (*Datura stramonium* var. *stramonium*) which started to grow on the edge of the trench during the excavation. Thorn-apple was used in medieval folk medicine. Its fruit pods, with long, hard thorns, were also used for less spectacular purposes: for preparing flax. Photo: Jens Heimdahl.

Apart from the potential of macrofossil analysis in the work of interpretation, a geological assessment of the sediment via direct geological and microscopic analyses in the field can help to enhance the source value of redeposited layers. As we saw above, the content of tertiary layers is generally of low source value for questions concerning dating and for identifying functions. A tertiary layer with a grain-size composition and organic content that is very similar to the soil occurring naturally in the local geology probably comes from the site and has only been redeposited to a small extent. If the material mainly consists of soils such as till, glaciofluvial material, or peat, it is probable that any finds come from the time when the earth was moved. The source value of the finds can thereby increase.

The stratigraphical sequence in the Konstantinopel block contained several sediments which are classed as "natural" in that they were formed by a geological process. The quaternary geologist was able to show, however, that "natural" sediment can be of interest for cultural history. An example of this is alluvial sediment formed by surface run-off. Processes that give rise to such sediments are easy to study in areas with exposed sediments, for example, piles of earth, gravel quarries, and dirt roads. When it rains or when meltwater flows, this leads to small alluvial formations and deposits, such as small deltas. In bodies of water, layers of fine-grained sediment are deposited. Alluvial sediments can contain many more remains of activities from the drained surface than from the original ground horizon where the alluvium originated. In this way a "naturally deposited" sediment can contain information about a lost area with traces of human impact. Remains in the form of macro- and microfossils, slag and forging sparks, charcoal, pieces of wood, bones, fish scales, and small finds in a sediment formed during a "natural process" can thus give answers to questions about activities and environments in the area from which they derived (Heimdahl *et al.* in prep.).

These examples are just a taster of the questions and problems that were discussed and ventilated in the course of the project. To sum up, we see the collaboration as an attempt at the development of archaeological and quaternary geological methodology, investigating the possibility of working continuously with quaternary geological methods in the field. The collaboration resulted in more discoveries and observations during the excavation, which sometimes led to new questions and priorities. The results also showed that new aspects of the interaction between man and the environment can be involved in archaeological interpretation and discussion.

The medieval town
- settlement development
in the Konstantinopel block

The results of the excavation of the Konstantinopel block will be published in two stages. The first report, which is expected to be finished in 2002, will present the basic processing and analysis of the source material. The final publication, on which work has not yet started, will contain a number of articles looking at various themes in greater depth and a summarizing

Fig. 5. Beer tap found in one of the houses and the cellar in the Konstantinopel block. Macrofossil finds of hops, hulled barley, bog myrtle, and meadowsweet show that beer was also brewed on the site. Photo: Rikard Hedvall, RAÄ.

compilation of the state of our archaeological knowledge of medieval Norrköping.

The first analysis of the material, as mentioned above, has led to a division into three periods which will be briefly summarized here. Period I represents a rural setting which can be dated to the end of the fourteenth century and the first half of the fifteenth century. The area was used for a variety of activities in the period. There were buildings on the site at times, but there are no traces of a permanent settlement structure in the form of plots or the like. At one stage there was some form of water installation, perhaps a mill, and a couple of furnaces with finds such as forging sparks and crucibles, indicating that metal crafts were pursued on the site. In addition, the area was flooded a number of times. What primarily characterizes the earliest period, however, is the traces of animal husbandry, which were also evident in the macrofossil analyses. They were dominated by manure and droppings, but there were also indications of ditches and marginal environments and a relatively large element of back-yard plants. There were nearly no collected or cultivated plants.

The next period has been dated to the second half of the fifteenth century and the first half of the sixteenth century. Period II is interpreted as representing a townyard. Settlement seems to have been regulated, and several buildings occur together simultaneously with courtyards and alleys. Indications of animal husbandry almost cease, but traces of terraces hint at attempts to reshape the topography. The macrofossils in period II mainly consist of collected and cultivated plants, but there was also a distinct element of street and back-yard environments. The waste material shows that slaughtering and fish cleaning, as well as beer making, took place on the site.

Period III has been dated to the second half of the sixteenth century. The area then had a clearly urban character with permanent and structured settlement. No animals were kept any longer, and the macrofossils show that the amount of collected and cultivated plants had decreased. Instead there was an element of exotic fruit. The period can be summed up as an urban environment with no direct proximity to animal husbandry or food preparation. The area was used by a smith (Karlsson *et al.* in prep.).

Development on the site seems to agree in part with the course of urbanization outlined for Norrköping. The town probably received a borough charter in the mid-fourteenth century. Despite this, the earliest period in the Konstantinopel block, which is mainly dated to the first half of the fifteenth century, is characterized by an agrarian environment. A likely interpretation of this is that even central parts of the town at this time still had a rural character. Townyards in regular plots did not come to this part of Norrköping until between the second half of the fifteenth century and the mid-sixteenth century. The town's great expansion phase in the second half of the sixteenth century is clearly seen in the palpably urban character of the area then. This phase constitutes our period III. In relation to the hypothesis formulated by Lindgren-Hertz, we may note that the results above all capture the medieval town but also the expansion phase, the dawn of Sweden's Age of Greatness. What may be surprising is that the earliest remains are not older than the end of the fourteenth century. It nevertheless con-

firms the interpretation that Norrköping in the Early Middle Ages should probably be regarded as a central place with several centres, and the spatial extent should not be sought only in the area that has been pointed out as the centre (Lindgren-Hertz this volume; Lindgren-Hertz 2001, pp. 281 ff.).

Conclusion

The aim of this article has been to describe the method we used in Norrköping to understand the course of urbanization in the Middle Ages and the early modern period. The experiences from Norrköping emphasize the importance of working with every town or place on the basis of its own specific circumstances, rather than assuming general processes. Our archaeological efforts in Norrköping have been driven by the ambition to work with a formulated overall hypothesis about the course of urbanization and to relate the results of the excavation to this in order to create meaningful and useful archaeological knowledge. Moreover, because it was possible to have continuity and to accumulate knowledge within one and the same excavating institution, and because two large urban investigations were started in two successive years, the conditions have been very good.

We hope that the results of our excavations of the Dalkarlen and Konstantinopel blocks will also shed new light on previous excavations in the town. The state of archaeological knowledge about Norrköping has improved considerably, but it is still important in the future to create new surveys of our knowledge and reformulate old hypotheses in order to identify new problem fields for tomorrow's excavations.

■ **Hanna Menander and Pär Karlsson**

References

Broberg, B. 1984. *Norrköping*. Riksantikvarieämbetets och Statens historiska museer rapport: Medeltidsstaden 50. Stockholm.

Ersgård, L. 2001. Människan vid kusten – fiskebebyggelse från Skagerack till Bottenhavet under senmedeltid och början av nyare tid. In Andrén, A., Ersgård, L., Wienberg, J. (eds.), *Från stad till land. En medeltidsarkeologisk resa tillägnad Hans Andersson.* Lund Studies in Medieval Archaeology 29. Stockholm.

Hållans, A.-M., Karlsson, P., and Tagesson, G. 1999. *Kvarteret Dalkarlen. Bebyggelse och industri i stormaktstidens Norrköping RAÄ 96.* Rapport UV Öst 1999:1. Arkeologisk undersökning. Norrköpings stad och kommun, Östergötland.

Harris, E. C., Brown III, M. R., Brown, G. J. 1993. *Practices of Archaeological Stratigraphy.* London.

Hedvall, R. (ed.) 2000. *Stadsgårdar i den senmedeltida stadsdelen Sanden, Vadstena.* Rapport UV Öst 2000:26. Linköping.

Heimdahl, J., Karlsson, P., Menander, H. In prep. Arkeologiskt och geologiskt samarbete i fält. Erfarenheter från den arkeologiska undersökningen i kv Konstantinopel, Norrköping. Manuscript for the publication from the 2001 conference of stratigraphy in Viborg.

Helmfrid, B. 1965. Norrköpings historia. Tiden 1568–1655. In Helmfrid, B., and Kraft, S. (eds.), *Norrköpings historia 5.* Stockholm.

Karlsson, P. 2000. Digital teknik och kontextuell metod – går det att kombinera? In Eriksdotter, G., Larsson, S., Löndahl, V. (eds.), *Att tolka stratigrafi. Det tredje nordiska stratigrafimötet. Åland 1999.* Meddelanden från Ålands högskola 11. Åbo.

Karlsson, P. In prep. Hus, tomter och kvarter i Tyskebacken. Manuscript for the final publication on the Dalkarlen block. Riksantikvarieämbetet.

Karlsson, P., and Menander, H. In prep. Kv Konstantinopel. Manuscript for the Daff report on the Konstantinopel block. Riksantikvarieämbetet.

Karlsson, P., Menander, H., and Westerlund, J. 2001. *En 1600-tals källare i kv Vattnet.* Rapport UV Öst 2001:60. Arkeologisk för- och slutundersökning. Norrköpings stad och kommun, Östergötland.

Larsson, S., and Johansson Hervén, C. 1998. Källmaterialsproduktion och förståelsehorisonter i stadsarkeologi. *Meta* 1998:2.

Larsson, S. 2000. *Stadens dolda kulturskikt. Lunda-arkeologins förutsättningar och förståelsehorisonter uttryckt genom praxis för källmaterialsproduktion 1890–1990.* Archaelogica Lundensia IX. Lund.

Lindeblad, K. 2000. Urbaniseringen i Östergötland. *Vetenskaplig verksamhetsplan för UV Öst. Arkeologiskt program 2000 – 2002.* Rapport UV Öst 2000:21. Linköping.

Lindgren-Hertz, L. 1999. *Mellan Landsförsamlingens kyrka och Strömmen. Kv Konstantinopel.* Rapport UV Linköping 1999:4. Arkeologisk förundersökning. Norrköpings stad och kommun, Östergötland.

Lindgren-Hertz, L. 2001. Speglingar av rumslig organisation. Norrköping i ljuset av mindre arkeologiska undersökningar. In Andrén, A., Ersgård, L., Wienberg, J. (eds.), *Från stad till land. En medeltidsarkeologisk resa tillägnad Hans Andersson.* Lund Studies in Medieval Archaeology 29. Stockholm.

Ljung, S. 1965. Norrköpings historia. Tiden intill 1568. In Helmfrid, B., and Kraft, S. (eds.), *Norrköpings historia 5.* Stockholm.

Menander, H. 2000. Ingen bonde ähr och nu snart som icke skall dricka tobach – en studie av kritpipors dateringsmöjligheter. In Eriksdotter, G., Larsson, S., Löndahl, V. (eds.), *Att tolka stratigrafi. Det tredje nordiska stratigrafimötet. Åland 1999.* Meddelanden från Ålands högskola 11. Åbo.

Menander, H. 2001. *Bebyggelsespår från stormaktstid i S:t Persgatan.* Rapport UV Öst 2001:12. Arkeologisk efterkontroll. Norrköpings stad och kommun, Östergötland.

Ringborg, E. 1921. *Kvarnarne i Norrköpings ström.* Norrköping.

Tagesson, G. 2000. Bodde dom därnere? Om kulturlagerbildning och avfallshantering i stormakttidens Norrköping. In Eriksdotter, G., Larsson, S., Löndahl, V. (eds.), *Att tolka stratigrafi. Det tredje nordiska stratigrafimötet. Åland 1999.* Meddelanden från Ålands högskola 11. Åbo.

Wallebom, U. In prep. Kvarteret Dalkarlen och Holmens Bruk – spåren efter 1600-talets industriella produktion. Manuscript for the final publication on the Dalkarlen block. Riksantikvarieämbetet.

Fig. 1. Motala is located at the point in Östergötland where Lake Vättern flows into the River Motala (Motala Ström). Since the Middle Ages the river has been used for mills and fishing. Photo: Jan Norrman, RAÄ.

Archaeological research into urbanization has mainly focused on the places that became towns in a formal sense during the Middle Ages, that is, the ones which received borough charters. The main reason for this is probably that only these places were published in the report series of "The Medieval Town". Parallel to the medieval towns there were a great many other places with different central functions for the surrounding population. They may have had several central functions or just one, in which case they are known as focal places. They may have functioned as assembly places for the district court, they may have had special ecclesiastical functions or served as administrative centres. What the majority of these places have in common is their manifest location in the landscape (see e.g. Aston 1995, pp. 44 ff.). To capture and discuss medieval central places, the importance of studying the function of the central place for the hinterland has been emphasized, that is to say, the way(s) in which they functioned as central places (Harrison 1997; Blomkvist 1982). The mining sites of central Sweden have been held up as examples of medieval central places. In several respects they functioned as towns, and had town-like settlement, even though they did not have a borough charter. Other examples of medieval central places that have been proposed are fishing stations and harbours along the coasts, where "feudal organizers" pursued trade without the involvement of the crown (Blomkvist 1982; Klackenberg 2001).

The present article deals with an example of a different type of central place, the medieval milling and fishing site of Motala. It is mentioned for the first time in written sources in 1288, when King Magnus Ladulås granted the lawman and councillor of the realm Knut Mattson a farm and fishing rights in Motala (Peterzén 1975, p. 85). This charter is the first in a long series showing the importance of the mills, fisheries, and plots of Motala throughout the Middle Ages. Motala shows several resemblances to the medieval town of Norrköping in eastern Östergötland (see Lindgren Hertz and Menander & Karlsson in this volume). The topographical locations of the two places are virtually identical, situated at either end of the River Motala, with mining areas to the north and rich plains to the south. For Norrköping too, the medieval written sources testify to extensive milling and permanent fishing in the Middle Ages. Norrköping emerges as a town in the mid-fourteenth century. Motala was not granted borough status until 1881. The fact that it never became a borough in the Middle Ages, as far as we know, is probably the main reason why Motala has hitherto been in the background in the discussion of the urbanization process in Östergötland.

This article seeks to highlight and describe Motala as a medieval central place and built-up area, and to some extent to discuss the prehistoric landscape. The starting point is the first two of the three criteria of urbanization presented in "The Medieval Town" project (Andersson 1978; Andersson 1990; see the chapter "Urban Archaeology in Östergötland" above). The source material consists of maps from the seventeenth and eighteenth centuries, written documents, and archaeological material. By combining these types of evidence, there is probably a good chance of discussing and identifying a number of different central places in the province and thus qualifying our picture of medieval Östergötland.

Where the forest meets the plain
The place-name Motala is composed of the two elements *mot* and *ala*. *Mot* means a place where roads meet, while *al* presumably means a shrine or temple. In other words, Motala would mean "the shrine at the crossroads" (Franzén 1982, p. 73). The place lies in a bay of Lake Vättern where the River Motala leaves it. Through Motala the old main road northwards to the mining districts passed via a bridge over the river. The road divided to the south of the bridge, continuing to the two medieval towns of Skänninge and Vadstena. In Motala the course of the river has partly changed with the construction of dams for the power station. Before it was regulated, the first waterfall was by the bridge, after which the river wound its way on to Lake Boren (Tham 1865, p. 681). On a point in Boren was the fortified manor of Ulfåsa, the seat of Birgitta Birgersdotter (Saint Birgitta) and Ulf Gudmarsson, councillor of the realm; it is recorded in writing for the first time in 1315 (Lovén 1996, p. 289).

Motala is in the hundred of Aska, on the boundary between two very different types of natural and cultural landscape. South of the River Motala the fertile plain opens out. To the north the landscape is dominated by forests and mountains, broken by a large number of small watercourses. On the plan the medieval parishes were small, with closely placed Romanesque churches, several of them built at the start of the twelfth century. The villages on the plain were large, with up to 15 homesteads, as we find them in the

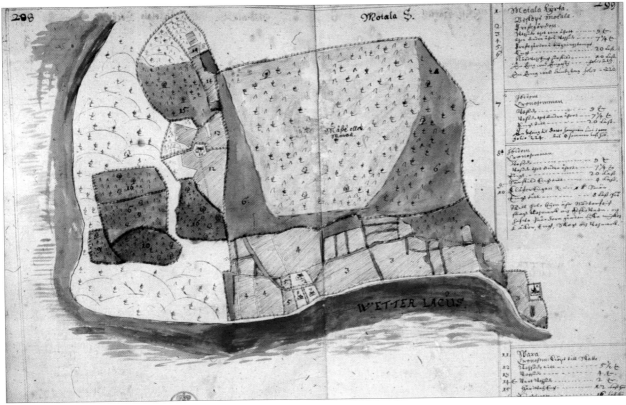

Fig. 2. The early maps show a very different picture of Motala from today's, when the town has spread over the former villages, fields, and pastures. This map from 1638 shows the village of Bispmotala (Bishop's Motala). Motala church can be seen in the south-east corner. The map is in the central office of the National Land Survey in Gävle.

oldest maps (Helmfrid 1962, p. 25). The plain also shows a wealth of archaeological material from the Late Iron Age and the Early Middle Ages. A concentration of Östergötland's early Christian runic burial monuments, Viking Age finds of precious metal, and runestones is found on the plain south and south-east of Motala (summarized by Lindeblad and Nielsen 1997, pp. 28 ff.; Nordanskog 1997). North of the River Motala the parishes are extensive and there are only two medieval churches, Godegård and Nykyrka, built slightly later than the ones on the plain. The rated value of the homesteads is always low, and most units in the seventeenth century were isolated farms (Arrhenius 1955). The northern parishes in Aska Hundred seem to have been mainly colonized in the Middle Ages in connec-

tion with the growth of mining. The mining districts of northern Östergötland are relatively unknown in both written and archaeological sources. The picture that can nevertheless be glimpsed is one of fairly large-scale iron production, with about fifty smelting houses (Nilsson 1990).

The earliest maps of the Motala district show rather dense settlement around the River Motala (fig. 3). There were a great many mills and fishing places on the river. On the stretch between the lakes Vättern and Boren, which is less than four kilometres long, there is a series of small falls. Water power has been harnessed since the Middle Ages. In 1725 there were no fewer than nineteen corn mills and five sawmills along the river (Kolsgård 1992, pp. 59 ff.). Beside the bridge, on the south bank of the river, lay Motala's southern village and Holm, with their mills and fisheries. On the north bank was the northern village of Motala and further to the east Hårstorp and Duvedal with mills and fisheries. West of the bridge, on the north shore of the bay, was the church and the freehold farm of Skattegården. A few hundred metres west of the church was the village of Bispmotala, meaning "Bishop's Motala". The same distinction between Bispmotala and Motala is made even in the earliest maps. All the villages and crofts are mentioned in the written sources from the Middle Ages. Today the modern town has spread over the older settlement.

Prehistoric outland?

The prehistory of the Motala district has been hardly discussed at all in the archaeological literature. On the few occasions when it has been described, it has been stated that the area, like the northern parts of the hundred, was not colonized until the Middle Ages. The district has been described as basically deserted. This assumption is chiefly based on the lack of fixed remains and on place-names (Peterzén 1981, p. 18; Peterzén in prep.). A recent survey just south-west of the present station area resulted in a series of newly discovered remains, including cemeteries from the Early and Late Iron Age. In connection with the survey, the medieval villages in the present urban area and a now vanished stone circle were also noticed (Nilsson 1996) (fig. 3). The stone circle is said to have stood at the place where the old roads from Skänninge and Vadstena met. Perhaps this is the very spot that gave Motala its name, the shrine at the crossroads? A look through the stray finds from Motala Parish shows that stray finds occur both within the present area of the town and in a few places to the north (fig. 3). Among the stray finds are above all a gold bracteate, a large ring brooch of silver, and a fragment of a runestone, all from the Late Iron Age. Besides these more spectacular finds there are some oval strike-a-lights, iron slag, whetstones, and a spindle whorl within and north of the present urban area (SHM inv. no. 9170). The latter find categories are rather more difficult to date, but

they could very well be settlement site finds from the Iron Age or Middle Ages.

The gold bracteate was found at the start of the twentieth century "in Motala by the northward railway", with no more precise statement as to the spot (Brate 1911, p. 167). Bracteates are an unusual category of find in Östergötland. They have previously been found at two other places, in Vadstena and north of Lake Roxen. In Scandinavia this category of object is dated to the Migration Period, and they are assumed to have circulated among the social elite. They were probably used when oaths of fidelity were sworn and in religious ceremonies. They are mostly found in graves or hoards. Bracteates with identical stamps have been used in research to define political alliances and groupings (Andrén 1991, pp. 247 ff.).

The fragment of a runestone was found at the end of the nineteenth century on the plot of the vicarage. It is on a noticeable rise a few hundred metres east of the church, close to the old main road through Motala. Yet another find from the Viking Age, a ring brooch of silver, was discovered in the River Motala in 1912. It is eleven centimetres in diameter and decorated with a stamped geometrical pattern.

Scandinavian Iron Age research in the last few years has discussed settlement hierarchies. The focus has above all been on the structures high up in the hierarchy, the places which on one way or another had central functions in relation to a hinterland. Attempts have also been made to characterize what distinguishes the location of these central places in the landscape, archaeological features, place-names, and the type of finds that one can expect to discover (see e.g. Fabech and Ringtved 1995). For places from the Late Iron Age, several indicators have been suggested which can very well be applied to the district around Motala. Among these are the favourable position for communications, the existence of sacred place-names ("the shrine at the crossroads"), and structural continuity in relation to properties owned by the crown and the nobility in the Middle Ages. The gold bracteate also fits neatly into an elite setting. Although the material

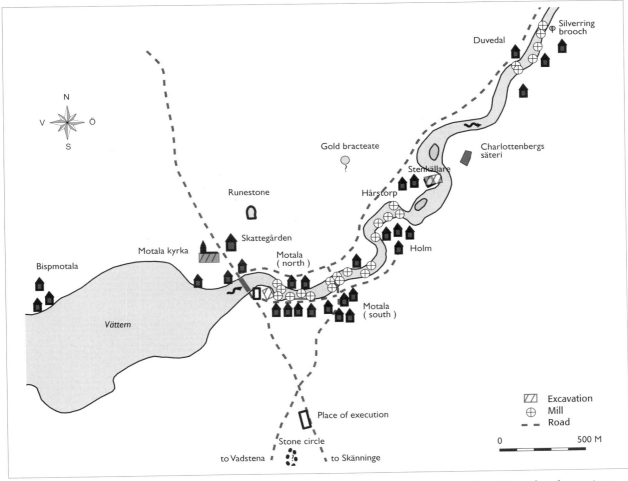

Fig. 3. The eighteenth-century village landscape and the numerous mills in the River Motala. The picture also shows stray finds from the Late Iron Age and the location of the three archaeological excavations conducted in today's Motala. Graphics: Lars Östlin, RAÄ.

from the Motala area is still too small, what we have mentioned above may be seen as an indication that the area should be regarded as important in the province, starting in the Late Iron Age, and was not deserted outland as has previously been assumed.

Motala in the written sources

The first time Motala is mentioned in writing is in 1288, when King Magnus Ladulås granted Knut Mattson, councillor of the realm, an estate in Motala with fishing rights. Motala is then mentioned several times in the medieval sources, above all in connection with changes of ownership of farms with mills and fixed fisheries. The landowners in Motala in the thirteenth and fourteenth centuries belonged to the aristocracy. There are hints in the written sources that certain properties in Motala were counted as belonging directly to the main estate of the Folkunga dynasty in Vadstena (Peterzén 1975). Here I shall discuss only a few of the written records, particularly those which can shed light on the character of Motala as a central place and a built-up area in the Middle Ages.

Fig. 4. Motala church and the bridge, Strömbron, from the eighteenth century. This bridge is probably in the same location as the medieval "Great Bridge". Photo: Karin Lindeblad, RAÄ.

Plots and attung units
- urban and agrarian?

Several of the medieval charters mention "plots" and "plot-men" in Motala. When the villages in the Motala district are mentioned, on the other hand, they are valued in *attung* figures. In the plains of Östergötland the attung or "eighth" was a unit of division used for regulating tenants' rents and a measure of the share of a farm in the village (Dovring 1980). In the charters discussed here, plots are mentioned in only a few cases, in the town of Norrköping. A charter from 1383 mentions the exchange of plots in Norrköping and plots in Motala. Norrköping at this time was an urban environment. The way of stating plots and plot-men, in both Norrköping and Motala, hints that both these places may have been perceived by contemporaries as similar settings.

The most interesting charter for a discussion of Motala as a central place and built-up area is from 1383 (Nordén 1917, no. 41). At that time the steward and lawman of Östergötland, Bo Jonsson (Grip), had come into possession of a large land holding in Motala Parish through an exchange with Marshall Karl Ulvsson. The charter was drawn up when Bo Jonsson exchanged these properties with Vadstena convent. The document mentions half an attung in Bispmotala, the bailiff's farm of Hårstorp, also valued in attung units, and several crofts in Motala Parish. There follows a list of the twenty plots in Motala owned by Bo Jonsson. The plots are not valued in attungs, as the agrarian units are, but are related to the men who occupy them, e.g. "the plot that Agmunda Skrap has". Among the names of plot holders we see above all Inge the sword-grinder, Jakob the smith, and Vaste the shoemaker. Their specialized crafts indicate that Motala was a town-like place. Finally, the charter mentions a large number of mills and fisheries that were included in the exchange of properties.

In connection with Queen Margareta's inquisition of 1405, plots in Motala are mentioned once again. This charter lists sixteen plots in Motala, including five belonging to the inheritance of Karl Karlsson, one plot belonging to the bishop of Linköping, and one belonging to the cathedral in Linköping. In addition, Motala church has three plots and the church in Vinnerstad is said to have a plot with no buildings. There is no mention of any craftsmen in this charter. On the other hand, it is clear that several ecclesiastical institutions were interested in owning plots in Motala.

Finally, a plot is mentioned in Bishop Brask's cadastre from the start of the sixteenth century. The property is said to be beside the Great Bridge (Peterzén 1981, p. 21). In the charter from 1383 one of the plot holders is called "Birger by the bridge". In other words, it seems as if the plots were beside the Great Bridge, in the same location as the present-day Strömbron (fig. 4).

The site of the Aska Hundred court
Motala is mentioned as the site of the hundred court for the first time in 1361. The wording of the charter suggests that the court was beside the church. Some time at the start of the 1370s the court moved permanently from the old site in Sjökumla to Motala (Peterzén 1981). The fact that the court moved to Motala reinforces the picture of Motala as a central place; the meetings of the court must have meant that a large number of people gathered here. The early maps show

a place of execution where the roads to Vadstena and Skänninge meet, and this could possibly be the site of the court (fig. 3).

Vadstena convent and Motala
In 1370 Birgitta Birgersdotter received the ratification for the foundation of her new convent in Vadstena. Through exchanges and donations of property, the convent became the country's biggest landowner, with properties above all concentrated in western Östergötland (Peterzén 1981, p. 21). Much of Motala Parish came into the possession of the convent. The mills and fisheries in Motala, along with those in Norrköping, were a very significant part of the convent's economy (Norborg 1958, p. 212). The mills seem to have mainly been used for grinding corn, but at the end of the Middle Ages there is a record of one being a sawmill. One of the farms in Motala at the end of the Middle Ages paid its tax in iron, which may indicate that there was a water-powered hammer forge. Other institutions in Östergötland had mills and fisheries in the River Motala, including the Cistercian abbey in Vreta and the bishop of Linköping (Peterzén 1981, pp. 26 ff.; Peterzén in prep.).

In the cadastres of Vadstena convent from the fifteenth century there are no data about holdings in Motala. For some reason, the heading for Motala Parish is followed in the document by a blank. In the cadastre from 1502 the convent's large possessions in Motala Parish are enumerated. It is stated that the convent owned ten farms in Motala village and a large number of mills and fisheries (Larsson 1971). The rents from these farms were paid in butter, and this is the first time that Motala itself is mentioned as an agrarian settlement; no plot holdings are mentioned in the cadastre.

Gustav Vasa's confiscation
With King Gustav Vasa's confiscation, virtually the whole of Motala Parish became crown property and would remain so for a long time to come (Peterzén 1975, p. 88). In the mid-sixteenth century Gustav Vasa began to erect stock farms, one in each hundred. These

farms were intended to be self-sufficient and to form the backbone of the new defence organizations. The place selected in Aska Hundred was Motala, no doubt because of the favourable location, the mills, and the rich fishing. The king had the bishop's land at his disposal, and the stock farm was founded south of the bridge, probably on the plot that Bishop Brask is stated to have owned beside the Great Bridge. There is no contemporary evidence for the location of the farm, but when Rantzau's troops burned the farm down during the Nordic Seven Years war, it is said to be south of the River Motala. Most of the fields, however, were on the north side of the bay, on the lands of Bispmotala (Peterzén 1981).

To sum up, it may be said that the written sources show that Motala had the character of a central place, with a church and a court, plots with no agrarian connection, and a large number of mills and fisheries. The names of some of the plot holders indicate a population with specialized craft occupations. The plots are listed in the charters in the same way as those in Norrköping, in other words, with the names of those who occupy them, unlike the agrarian units which are divided into attung units or called crofts. The large number of plots shows that Motala, at least at the end of the fourteenth century and the start of the fifteenth century, may be defined as built-up, that is to say, the settlement here was denser than in the villages in the surrounding countryside. When Vadstena convent then became the predominant landowner in Motala, settlement seems more to have consisted of ordinary agrarian units, and the mills and

fisheries appear to have been the convent's primary interests. It is possible that the craftsmen had to move to Vadstena.

Archaeological investigations

Only a few archaeological investigations have been carried out in the Motala district. The reasons for this are that no prehistoric monuments were registered here and that the place has not been considered a medieval central place and built-up area. Two excavations have been conducted beside the only surviving medieval stone buildings, Motala church and the Hårstorp farm. In 2000 there was a small-scale excavation at the bridge, Strömbron (see fig. 3). These excavations will be described briefly.

Church and chapel

Motala church is on a distinct rise near Lake Vättern and the bridge over the River Motala. It is first mentioned in writing in 1361. It acquired its present appearance in the 1680s and the 1770s (fig. 5). The church had no tower until the mid-nineteenth century; before that there was a separate bell tower. When the church was restored in 1952–1953 it was subjected to an archaeological investigation. This showed that the masonry of an older Romanesque church was preserved in the southern part of the present nave. Under the floor were the surviving foundation walls of the older church, which was much smaller. The

Fig. 5. In the 1660s the Romanesque church in Motala was extended to the east and south. Drawing: Elias Brenner 1669.

earlier church was about 20 m long and 6.6 m wide, built of cut limestone "of fairly large format". Based on the appearance of the masonry, the suggested date of the church is the first half of the thirteenth century. The church had a chancel and apse but no tower. Finds of shaped brick indicate that the church was vaulted. In the southern wall of the nave there were traces of two doors, one into the western part and one into the chancel. Between these doors there were traces of a window (Cnattingius 1964).

The churches in the large forest parishes north of Motala, Nykyrka and Godegård, appear to have been built in the second half of the thirteenth century, and they have neither tower nor apse. The church in Motala is closer to the tradition of church building that prevailed in western Östergötland in the twelfth century, with the exception that the church was not given a tower in the Middle Ages. Several of the churches on the plain are considered to have originally been built as private estate churches. The church in Motala is likely to have originally been one of these, erected by a local magnate.

In Motala there has also been a chapel dedicated to Saint Birgitta. It is mentioned in Bishop Brask's list of "chapels without priests" and is stated to have been beside the bridge (e.g. Fröjmark 1990, p. 143 and references cited there). Birgitta was canonized in 1391 and the chapel is likely to have been built some time after that date. It was probably demolished at the Reformation, and no trace of it survives today.

The islet with the stone building at Hårstorp

In 1921 a medieval stone building was excavated at the farm of Hårstorp (fig. 3). The excavation was occasioned by the construction of a dam for a power station in the River Motala. Today the whole of Hårstorp is under water in a lake called Hårstorpssjön. The manor of Hårstorp is mentioned for the first time in written sources in 1296, when it was owned by Abjörn Sixtensson, a man who later became councillor of the realm and steward (drots). The written sources suggest that Hårstorp was one of Abjörn Sixtensson's

manors (Peterzén 1975, p. 85). When Bo Jonsson (Grip) made his great exchange of properties with Vadstena convent in 1383, the estate was called a bailiff's farm (brytegård). The art historian Christian Lovén believes that the farm had then declined in importance and that the only hint of any fortification is in a charter of 1307. The estate is also mentioned in 1405 when it is listed as a "king's third" (kungstreding), that is, the king's share of the common land (Lovén 1996, p. 426). Hårstorp is mentioned in the cadastre of Vadstena convent from 1502, when it was a considerable farm paying a rent far in excess of that of the other farms in Motala (Larsson 1971).

The excavations concentrated on the ruins of a cellar room which was on an islet 50 metres long in the River Motala, with a moat dug facing the land. The building was 10 by 7 m, with a partially sunken cellar. It probably had an upper storey of wood or stone with a hall. Lundberg would compare the architecture with the building tradition of bishops Brask and Tidemansson (Lundberg 1932, p. 223). According to this interpretation, the building in Hårstorp would have been constructed at the end of the fifteenth century or the start of the sixteenth. An alternative interpretation of the age of the building could be that it was erected in the fourteenth century. It was common at that time that manors moved out of the villages to locations of this type (Hansson 2001, pp. 256 ff.). Together with the written sources, which suggest that the estate was fortified in the fourteenth century, this is a more reasonable interpretation in my opinion.

The finds from the excavation are fairly anonymous, with the exception of two coins which were found in the layer on the floor in the cellar, both from the mid-sixteenth century. Otherwise the majority of the finds are various metal objects, building details such as keyhole plates, nails, hasps, and edge mountings (SHM inv. no. 16896). The finds that are datable apart from the coins are some sherds of stoneware and a horseshoe. These do not contradict the date of the coins (pers. com. Kerstin Engdahl, Museum of National Antiquities). A thick fire layer covered the

Fig. 6. In 2000 a small-scale excavation was carried out on the promontory where Lake Vättern flows into the River Motala. Photo: Jan Norrman, RAÄ.

remains of the building. Some of the finds also showed signs of fire. It is therefore reasonable to envisage that the cellared house at Hårstorp burned down at the end of the sixteenth century or the start of the seventeenth, but we can never attain full certainty about when it was built. On the other hand, one can conclude that the estate of Hårstorp was a significant point in the Motala district as early as the thirteenth or fourteenth century. It is also worth nothing that the exchanges comprising plots in Motala also include Hårstorp.

At the bridge

In three autumn months of 2000 a small-scale total excavation was conducted near the Strömbron bridge (see fig. 3). It covered an area of about 100 m² and also included an introductory marine archaeological investigation in the River Motala (Carlsson *et al.* in prep.). The investigations are not completed, so the interpretation of the results should be regarded as hypotheses for the coming two seasons that the investigations are expected to continue.

The excavation area is at a very strategic point in the landscape from the point of view of communications, on the eastern side of the promontory that divides Lake Vättern from the River Motala. The waters of the river here are described as calm in comments on the map from 1718. The surveyor noted that this part of the river was used for fishing. This is the location today of Strömbron, a stone-vaulted bridge from the eighteenth century, probably identical with the "Great Bridge" mentioned in the Middle Ages. Medieval documents also mention plots by the bridge, probably at Strömbron, but it is of course impossible to say whether they lay north or south of the bridge. In 1383, as we have seen, there is a record of a plot occupied by "Birger by the bridge". A Birgittine chapel is also said to have stood beside the bridge (see above). The roads southwards from the bridge led to Skänninge and Vadstena while the north road led towards the province of Närke. In the earliest map from 1639 there is a building called Kungshuset (Kings' House) beside the bridge, probably identical with a building later known as Duke Johan's hunting castle, which survives today as a ruined cellar. This is also the location of the stock farm that Gustav Vasa established in Motala in the sixteenth century. Maps from the eighteenth century mark a couple of buildings on the same site as Kungshuset, but the name now is Motala Inn. On both maps the area we excavated is marked as arable land. The inn survived until the 1960s when the national road 50 was built straight through Motala and the inn was in the way.

The excavation area is only a couple of metres from the River Motala, on a gentle slope towards the east; during the twentieth century it was a garden. The occupation layers were up to a metre thick, with an elusive stratigraphy consisting of layers and features ranging from the Late Mesolithic to modern times. It was hard to distinguish one layer from another since they all mainly consisted of brown, sandy humus. The boundaries between the layers should therefore not be perceived as exact as regards either extent or dating. The two earliest layers can be dated to the Mesolithic, so they will not be considered here. The latest layer was a levelling layer, probably spread in the 1990s. The content of two of the intermediate layers is most interesting for our purposes. Over the Mesolithic layer there was a sooty layer of humus containing occasional pieces of brick. In the northern part of the trench were four hearths, of which only one was visible in the trench wall, some small pits, and a gully. In the filling of one of the hearths there was forging slag and a small piece of bronze plate, leading to the interpretation as a forge for ironworking. In a smaller pit there was also a cutting of bronze. The smith may also have worked with bronze casting. The hearth has been dated to AD 670 – 860. The function of the other two hearths has not been determined, but two of them have been radiocarbon-dated, giving the following results: AD 140 – 170, 210 – 380, and 400 – 540.

The long time over which the layer was formed is difficult to break down into narrower sequences. The layer contained finds which can be generally dated to the Iron Age and Middle Ages. At present the medieval objects cannot be associated with any features or structures; they should be interpreted as having been thrown out of adjacent parts of the promontory. The finds include other objects which can be associated with forging: iron slag and a preform for a fire steel. One of the pieces of slag has been ^{14}C-dated to AD 1220 – 1310, 1350 – 1390, which hints at site continuity as regards ironworking. The material also contains a couple of potsherds of a general Iron Age character, yet another couple of bronze foil pieces, a sherd from a stoneware jug (CI ware), a padlock key, a fragment of a medieval comb and a fragmentary coin dated 1275–1290. It is worth noting that none of the date-indicating objects is later than the end of fourteenth century. In the layer on top of the one containing traces of forging there were remains which can be interpreted as a change in the use of the area. There was a context interpreted as a cultivated patch with a characteristic horizon of small stones in the lower part. Towards the river there was a line of fist-sized stones, interpreted as ploughed-up stones laid at the side of the patch. The layer contained a set of potsherds (BII:4) ware which can be dated from the end of the Middle Ages to the eighteenth century. The finds also include a coin from 1674. The interpretation of the area as arable land agrees well with the information on the early maps, where the area is marked as arable.

The small-scale marine archaeological investigation in the river beside the site discovered a row of about ten piles from the north bank of the river towards the excavation area. Whether the piles continued all the way across the river must remain an open question since the river has been dredged in modern times. Two of the piles have been dendrochronologically dated to the 1080s. The dated piles were of oak, quarter-trunks with pointed ends. It is difficult to interpret the structure, as several alternatives are conceivable. In view of the excellent conditions for fishing at the site, it may be envisaged that the row of piles was used for the attachment of nets or traps. If so, this would be the earliest evidence of the important fisheries mentioned in the medieval charters. Another interpretation could be that the structure served as a barrier against boats entering the river, a common phenomenon in this period (Lovén 1996, pp. 449 ff.). The row of piles in the River Motala may of course have had both functions, perhaps also being used as a bridge across the river. The function will have to be left open for the time being, but the fact remains that someone thought that he had the right, and evidently had the will, to block all or part of the river at the end of the eleventh century.

Summing up the as yet preliminary results, we see that the promontory by the bridge was used from the Late Iron Age for forging, probably connected to a farm by the bridge. In the 1080s, parts of the River Motala, or perhaps all of it, were blocked at the excavation site. The function of the structure is still uncertain, but it may be regarded as the first of the many structures that set their stamp on the river in the Middle Ages. Forging on the excavation site continued into the Middle Ages, and it is not wholly unreasonable to imagine that this is the site of one of the craft plots mentioned in the written sources. This work ceased

at the end of the Middle Ages, after which the site was used as arable land, as it was in the earliest maps. The change may possibly be associated with a restructuring of land use when Vadstena convent became the dominant landowner in Motala.

Conclusion

In this article I have tried to highlight what we know about Motala, describing it as a medieval central place and built-up area on the basis of the first two criteria used in "The Medieval Town" project. By applying these to historical and archaeological source material, along with early maps, one finds that there is good reason to describe Motala as both a central place and a built-up area. In addition, I have tried to describe and interpret the landscape that preceded the medieval place.

Earlier research has claimed that the Motala district, like the northern parts of the hundred, were mainly colonized in the Middle Ages. In recent years, new surveys have been conducted in the south-west part of the town. These have yielded a number of formerly unregistered ancient monuments, including cemeteries from the Early and Late Iron Age. The ongoing excavation in Motala also clearly shows the occurrence of forging beside the bridge. The stray finds also argue against the late colonization of the area. They include, above all, a gold bracteate, a large ring brooch of silver, and a fragment of a runestone, all dating from the Late Iron Age. The finds, together with the interpretation of the place-name as "the shrine at the crossroads" and the favourable position for communications, actually hint that the area around the River Motala functioned at an early stage as a central place for the surrounding countryside. It seems as if the area belong to the rich plains south of the river rather than to the forests to the north.

As the start of the thirteenth century a Romanesque church was erected in Motala, probably on the lands of the village of Bispmotala. The church underwent an archaeological investigation when it was restored at the start of the 1950s. It was found that the walls of the nave of the earlier church were incorporated in the later one; some of the foundation walls of the older church also survived under the floor. It follows the early Romanesque building tradition of the plains south of Motala, where several churches were private churches attached to a magnate's estate. The church in Motala, and the size of the parish, differed strikingly from the later churches without towers and apses in the forest parishes north of Motala.

Particularly from the end of the fourteenth century and the start of the fifteenth century, there are a number of written records showing that Motala differed in terms of function and topography from the surrounding countryside; in other words, it can be described as a built-up central place. This should be viewed against the background of the favourable location on the river which provided fish and power, on the boundary between two very different natural resource areas. The place may have been used for reloading and processing iron from the mining area north of Motala, which was then emerging. The written sources let us glimpse a settlement which, like the contemporary town of Norrköping, was divided into plots. The occupants of some of the plots in Motala at the end of the fourteenth century were professional craftsmen. There are records of Inge the sword-grinder, Jakob the smith, and Vaste the shoemaker. The ongoing excavation by the bridge shows that forging was pursued here in the Late Iron Age and until the end of the Middle Ages. The smithing activities could possibly be associated with the plots beside the bridge. Other functions indicating specialization here are the large number of mills and the fisheries. The owners of these and of the plots belonged to the aristocracy of the day, with well-known names like the steward and lawman of Östergötland, Bo Jonsson (Grip), and Marshall Karl Ulfsson (Sparre av Tofta). Ecclesiastical institutions in Östergötland also owned plots and fisheries in Motala; these include the bishop of Linköping, the cathedral in Linköping, and Alvastra abbey. At the end of the fourteenth century Motala also became the site of the court of Aska Hundred. The court assemblies, the various activities at the mills,

and the chapel of Saint Birgitta along the pilgrim route to Vadstena must have meant that considerable numbers of people came to Motala at certain times of the year.

During the Middle Ages Hårstorp was the most important farm around the River Motala. The house had a stone cellar with an upper storey of timber or stone. It was in an isolated location on an islet in the river, a kind of location which became common in the fourteenth century. The first time the estate is mentioned it was owned by the steward Abjörn Sixtensson (Sparre av Tofta). It later belonged to Bo Jonsson (Grip) but came into the possession of Vadstena convent in the Late Middle Ages. In the exchanges of property that include details of plots in Motala, they are always mentioned together with Hårstorp. The plots were possibly subject to the manor in the same way as the tenant farms and crofts.

At the end of the fourteenth century and the start of the fifteenth, Vadstena convent became the main owner of the whole of Motala Parish. According to the cadastre from the start of the sixteenth century, the convent owned not only a large number of mills and fisheries, but also ten farms in the village of Motala. Motala itself is described for the first time as if it were an agrarian village. Hårstorp seems to have still been the most important farm around the River Motala. The rents from this farm far exceed those of the other farms in Motala. King Gustav Vasa's confiscation at the start of the sixteenth century meant that virtually all of Motala Parish became crown property, as it would remain for a long time. A stock farm was established in Motala at the southern abutment of the bridge and in Bispmotala.

In the written sources the character of Motala as a central place is most distinct at the end of the fourteenth century, before Vadstena convent became the major landowner. As far as we know, Motala never became a town in the Middle Ages in an administrative and legal sense. A possible explanation for this is that ownership was dominated above all by the secular nobility, as well as by ecclesiastical institutions, and

Fig. 7. A view of Motala when the Göta Canal was constructed. The inn stood at the southern abutment of the Strömbron bridge, while the church is visible on the north side. This painting by an unknown artist is in Motala Museum.

that the king, who was the chief founder of towns in the Middle Ages, had little opportunity and perhaps not even the will to establish a town here. Hypothetically, the establishment of the plots with craftsmen in Motala was associated with the big noble farms of Hårstorp and Ulvåsa, which belonged for periods to the king's leading men, and that trade and craft in Motala could be pursued with the king's consent.

The tendencies to urbanization were curbed when the convent became the biggest landowner in the area, founding the town of Vadstena less than twenty kilometres away. A similar explanation has been proposed for Hästholmen (Klackenberg 1984). The town was in a good natural harbour on Lake Vättern, close to the Cistercian abbey of Alvastra. Around 1300 the place is mentioned in writing as a *villa forensis*, a town, unlike Motala. Hästholmen shows sign of urbanization in the fourteenth century, with mercantile functions, a court, and the castle of Hästholmen which was the centre of a fief. A suggested hypothesis is that Alvastra abbey was of crucial influence for the development of Hästholmen into an urbanized place and that it can be compared with the abbots' and bishops' towns that are known from north-west Europe. Around 1400 Vadstena became the new and dominant place in western Östergötland, and Hästholmen then seems to have declined in importance. It was not until the mid-nineteenth century that Hästholmen and Motala once again enjoyed an upswing when shipping on Lake Vättern became more vigorous as a result of steamboat traffic and the construction of the Göta Canal.

■ **Karin Lindeblad**

Note

This article is a revised and abridged version of an article previously published in 2001 in *Från stad till land: En medeltidsarkeologisk resa tillägnad Hans Andersson*, ed. Anders Andrén *et al.* (Lund Studies in Medieval Archaeology 29, Stockholm).

References

Andersson, H. 1978. *Urbaniseringsprocessen i det medeltida Sverige*. Riksantikvarieämbetets och Statens historiska museer rapport: Medeltidsstaden 7. Stockholm.

Andersson, H. 1990. *Sjuttiosex medeltidsstäder – aspekter på stadsarkeologi och medeltida urbaniseringsprocess i Sverige och Finland*. Riksantikvarieämbetets och Statens historiska museer rapport: Medeltidsstaden 76. Stockholm.

Andrén, A. 1972. Guld och makt – en tolkning av de skandinaviska guldbrakteaternas funktion. In Fabech, C., and Ringtved, J. (eds.), *Samfundsorganisation og Regional Variation. Norden i romersk jernalder og folkevandringstid. Beretning fra 1. nordiske jernaldersymposium på Sandbjerg Slot 11 – 15 april 1989*. Jysk Arkæologisk Selskabs Skrifter XXVII. Århus.

Arrhenius, O. 1955. Åkermarkens urgamla hävd. *Fornvännen 50*.

Aston, M. 1985. *Interpreting the Landscape. Landscape Archaeology in Local Studies*. London.

Blomkvist, N. 1982. Samhällsekonomi och medeltida stadstillväxt – till frågan om generella förklaringar. *Bebyggelsehistorisk Tidskrift 3*.

Brate, E. 1911. *Östergötlands runinskrifter. Sveriges runinskrifter* 2. Stockholm.

Cnattingius, B. 1964. Motala kyrka. *Linköpings stifts kyrkor. Aska och Dals kontrakt*. Linköping.

Dovring, F. 1980. Attung. *Kulturhistoriskt lexikon för nordisk medeltid* 1. Copenhagen.

Fabech, C., and Ringtved, J. 1995. Magtens geografi i Sydskandinavien – om kulturlandskap, produktion og bebyggelsesmønster. In Resi, H. G. (ed.), *Produksjon og samfunn*. Om erverv, spesialisering og bosetning i Norden i 1. årtusen e.Kr. Varia 30. Oslo.

Franzén, G. 1982. *Ortnamn i Östergötland*. Stockholm.

Fröjmark, A. 1990. Kyrkornas skyddshelgon i Östergötland "västanstång" under tidig medeltid. In Dahlbäck, G. (ed.), *I Heliga Birgittas trakter. Nitton uppsatser om medeltida samhälle och kultur i Östergötland "västanstång"*. Stockholm.

Hansson, M. 2001. Huvudgårdar och herravälden. En studie i smålänsk medeltid. Lund Studies in Medieval Archaeology 25. Lund.

Harrison, D. 1997. Centralorter i historisk forskning om tidig medeltid. Callmer, J., and Rosengren, E. (eds.), *"…gick Grendel att söka det höga huset…" Arkeologiska källor till aristokratiska miljöer i Skandinavien under yngre järnåldern*. Slöinge Projektet 1. Hallands Länsmuseers Skriftserie 9. Halmstad.

Helmfrid, S. 1962. *Östergötland Västanstång. Studien über die ältere Agrarlandschaft und ihre Genese*. Meddelanden från Geografiska institutionen vid Stockholms universitet 140.

Klackenberg, H. 1984. *Hästholmen*. Riksantikvarieämbetets och Statens historiska museer rapport: Medeltidsstaden 59. Stockholm.

Klackenberg, H. 2001. Capella Pata. In Andrén, A., Ersgård, L., Wienberg, J. (eds.), *Från stad till land. En medeltidsarkeologisk resa tillägnad Hans Andersson*. Lund Studies in Medieval Archaeology 29. Stockholm.

Kolsgård, S. 1992. Motala ström – kraftgivare sedan medeltiden. In Castensson, R. (ed.), *Kraften ur Motala ström*. Linköping.

Larsson, A. 1971. *Vadstena klosters två äldsta jordeböcker*. Samlingar utgivna av Svenska fornskriftssällskapet 245. Uppsala.

Lindeblad, K., and Nielsen, A.-L. 1997. Centralplatser i västra Östergötland 200 – 1200 e Kr. Ett första försök till rumslig analys. In Larsson, L., *Riksväg 50. Arkeologisk utredning etapp 1. RAÄ rapport. UV Linköping 1997:3*. Linköping.

Lovén, C. 1996. *Borgar och befästningar i det medeltida Sverige*. Stockholm.

Lundberg, E. 1932. Hårstorp. En byggnad från 1500-talet och dess medeltida fränder. In Thordeman, B. (ed.), *Arkeologiska Studier tillägnade H.K.H. Kronprins Gustaf Adolf*. Svenska Fornminnesföreningen. Stockholm.

Nilsson, O. 1990. Östergötlands norra bergslager. En översikt. In Dahlbäck, G. (ed.), *I Heliga Birgittas trakter. Nitton uppsatser om medeltida samhälle och kultur i Östergötland "västanstång".* Stockholm.

Nilsson, P. 1996. *Arkeologisk utredning etapp 1. Nytt dubbelspår Godegård–Mjölby. Delsträckan Motala C–Fågelstad.* RAÄ rapport. UV Linköping 1996:40. Linköping.

Norborg, L.-A. 1958. *Storföretaget Vadstena kloster. Studier i senmedeltida godspolitik och ekonomiförvaltning.* Lund.

Nordén, A. 1917. *Norrköpings medeltid. Ett Diplomatarium Norcopense.* Stockholm.

Peterzén, I. 1975. Från stormansbesittning till klostergods. Om Motalas medeltida ägostruktur. *Meddelanden från Östergötlands och Linköpings Stadsmuseum.*

Peterzén, I. 1981. Det medeltida Motala. In Bolinder, J. (ed.), *Motala 100 år.* Motala.

Tham, W. 1855. *Beskrifning över Linköpings län.* Stockholm.

Unpublished sources

Carlsson, T., Gruber, G., and Lindeblad, K. Rapport RAÄ, UV Öst. In prep.

Nordanskog, G. 1997. Den tidiga kungamakten i Östergötland. Territorialisering, exploatering och maktanspråk. D-uppsats. Department of Medieval Archaeology, Lund University.

Peterzén, I. Manuscript for the centennial publication on Motala. Motala Centralarkiv.

Statens Historiska Museum (SHM), inventarieförteckning.

Land survey documents at the National Land Survey in Linköping

Motala Parish, doc. no. and year

D71-8:1	1684
D71-8:2	1722
D71-19:1	1708
D71-32:1	1773
D71-34:1	1703
D71-49:1	1713
D71-49:2	1712
D71-49:3	1717
D71-49:7	1781
D71-49:9	1827

Vinnerstad Parish doc. no. and year

D5:192-3, 196	1636
D128-6:1	1713
D5:192-3	1636
D128-6:1	1713
D5:197	1636
D128-6:1	1713

Space

Urban archaeology in Sweden has changed in the last twenty years. The great wave of town excavations has gradually ebbed away; we will never again see a similar archaeological "gold rush", never more will new source material be produced at such a rapid speed as we saw then. A time of positivist euphoria has been replaced by a period giving an opportunity for reflection, with external demands for clearer motivation for urban development, meaning fewer excavations, and with internal possibilities for formulating problems.

At the same time, interest in the towns has shifted noticeably from the question of urbanization, that is, how and when towns emerged, and the role of towns in the growth of royal power and the Swedish state. Parallel to the shift of interest in the cultural sciences – from the grand history and large, faceless processes in society to the little, individual, ambiguous history – the role of the town as a living space and a social project has attracted increased interest.

In this article the searchlight will be on spatial aspects. The great methodological advantage of archaeology in being able to compare the spatial occurrence and distribution of various phenomena has made space into an important concept. Not very long ago, however, it was mainly perceived as a neutral stage for people in bygone times. Since the Second World War and above all in the 1960s–70s, the focus has been on people's relationship to the environment and the topography, with analyses of economically oriented human activity and its adjustment to ecology and natural conditions (Knapp and Ashmore 1999, pp. 2 ff.).

In the 1980s–90s, on the other hand, space has increasingly been regarded as subjective, as a *cultural* landscape. Whereas earlier research mainly concentrated on the objective and measurable values of space, new spatial studies are trying to highlight space from the perspective of the individual. A central idea is that people create their own living environment, which exists and acquires meaning only through human action. There are no natural spaces; space is created by people. By means of boundaries, classification, naming, architecture, and so on, we create space and boundaries in a boundless world. We orient ourselves with the use of a set of concepts to create a personal and individual order through associations, memories, names, and by our way of being in and using space (Parker Pearson and Richards 1994; Tilley 1994, pp. 7 ff.).

In this tradition the emphasis is on *acting* rather than *behaving*. Through myths people are able to create an understanding of and orientation in the world, with their own house and hearth being the centre and the point of departure. Space is perceived and learned through a categorization and classification that mainly proceeds from the human body through concepts such as left/right, up/down, male/female. Space and organization can be studied as an expression of the individual or the social group. By studying space and architecture, the social relations embedded in space can be analysed (e.g. Hillier and Hanson 1984; Gurevich 1985, pp. 41 ff.; Harrison 1996; Kealhofer 1999).

But space is not just a passive mirror of social relations between people. Space can be deliberately shaped

Fig. 1. The civic seal of Linköping from 1360. Photo: National Archives.

Fig. 2. Linköping from the air. The town centre is still dominated by the cathedral and some surrounding ecclesiastical institutions. Despite the ambition to be a modern high-tech centre, the town plan still bears witness to its medieval history. Photo: Jan Norrman, RAÄ.

in order to influence behaviour, as in the case of mental hospitals and prisons, and also in the conscious use of space that we find, for example, in monasteries. Here the ideologically permeated shaping of the architecture is a device for influencing and reshaping the people who live in and visit the buildings, designed to regulate the encounter between people (e.g. Bartlett 1994; Foucault 1998; Gilchrist 1994).

The idea of space and architecture as a means of power with the ability to influence has not gone uncontradicted, however. According to other scholars, space is influenced more by people's behaviour than the reverse. Architecture proposes or suggests a particular behaviour, but it cannot determine our actions. This

viewpoint can of course be debated, but the crucial point is the problematization of the relationship between power and resistance, between influence and submission. With this interpretation, space is not just a reflection of the social organization. Activity, behaviour, and social relations are produced, controlled, and reproduced in space. The visible space is essentially a meeting between people, the medium through which social relations are produced and reproduced (Giddens 1984, p. 362). With this outlook, a goal of archaeological analysis is to demonstrate changes within one and the same space in order to study fundamental changes between people in society (Grenville 1997, pp. 20 ff., 2000).

The basis for a future analysis of Linköping is that the town is a meeting place for different relations, and that changes between these relations can be studied over time and in space. To sum up, space can be used as an analytical tool to discern these relations. The urban space is regarded as the stage on which these relations are actively concretized and manifested, often in symbolically charged form. At the same time, the urban space is regarded as one of several places in which the social structures are embedded. Space is not a mirror of society but is itself society.

The example

The present article is a presentation of a doctoral dissertation, a body of empirical material, and some working methods. The dissertation examines the archaeological material from a specific town – medieval Linköping – with the aim of studying social relations in medieval society and how these are expressed in material culture and spatial structure. The study comprises the economic, social, and ideological relations between the church and the town, with examples and empirical material from the diocesan capital of Linköping *c.* 1000 – 1700 (Tagesson 2002).

The questions I ask of this material, however, have varied over the years. The starting point was my curiosity about the results of some major excavations at the end of the 1980s, when the archaeological evidence indicated a development in the town which differed from the usual picture. The foundation was a traditional archaeological analysis of settlement development and material culture, and the settlement was interpreted as having got off to a tentative start in the fourteenth century, but with a noticeable growth around 1400. This picture could be contrasted with a hitherto prevailing older picture based on written sources, whereby the town was interpreted as an extremely ancient ecclesiastical central place, followed by a development into a town in the thirteenth century and with continuous development until the Reformation (Feldt and Tagesson 1997; Kraft 1975).

One way of explaining the discontinuous history suggested by the archaeological material was to try to study the town in relation to the ecclesiastical economy. The idea is that it is possible to seek an explanation for the development of the town in the relation between the town and the burghers on the one hand and the cathedral, the chapter, and the bishop on the other. By studying different types of source material at different levels, it should be possible to capture different hierarchies in society and shed fuller light on the decisive factors (Tagesson and Wigh 1994; Tagesson 1997).

In recent years the interest has increasingly been shifted to the relationship between the people in the town and how social role-play and strategies can be discovered in the extant source material. Here it is not just economic circumstances that are important, but also how identity and group affiliation are expressed and configured in the form of material culture and spatial structure through streets and alleys, plots and their content, architecture, and so on.

To be able to handle a large body of archaeological source material, the main quality of which could be said to be its spatiality, its quantity and distribution in the town, GIS (geographical information systems) have proved to be very useful. This combines databases and maps in an integrated way. A fundamental method for the study of the medieval town of Linköping has been to create an excavations register (SR) and a register of buildings (BR) following the model of "The Medieval Town" project (Andersson 1979, 1990).

The two registers have been linked in the GIS to maps comprising a modern digitized base map, a digital version of the oldest plot map from 1696, and all the archaeological investigations represented by the extent of the trenches (SR) and all the known or surviving stone houses (BR). These are available in the GIS as several different digital map layers which can be combined as necessary. Further layers of a more analytical kind are, for example, archaeological information such as the courses of earlier roads, buildings, wells, finds, etc., with an infinite number of possible combinations.

The advantage of GIS is the possibility of combining a quantity of information, giving an easy and clear way to compare the information from an archaeological investigation with earlier excavations in the same area or with the location in relation to early maps. The results of the excavation can thus be evaluated and understood in a spatial context in a more integrated way than was formerly possible.

Plots

The most important thing in this context, however, is to regard the GIS as a technical instrument, not as a method in itself. The method that is used, on the other hand, is of a more traditional kind, which could be described as *retrospective*. Based on the oldest plot map from 1696, attempts are made to analyse the town plan and its different chronological phases. The map of 1696 has been regarded as a good example of

the medieval town plan, but even if we can assume that in parts it goes back to and reflects an earlier town plan, we should regard the map as applying only to the time when it was drawn. The town plan of 1696 is a product of many centuries of development, thus bearing its own history (fig. 3, 4). Different phases can be discerned by a combination of written sources, formal analysis, and archaeological evidence (see Lilley 2000 and works cited there about British studies of town plans).

The oldest plot map from 1696 marks all the plots and their owners. Alongside streets and alleys and public places, plots are the most important elements in the urban space, corresponding to private pieces of physical land, whether with or without buildings. In the Middle Ages a distinction was made between a

Fig. 3. The town plan from 1696, the oldest testimony of the plots and their inhabitants.

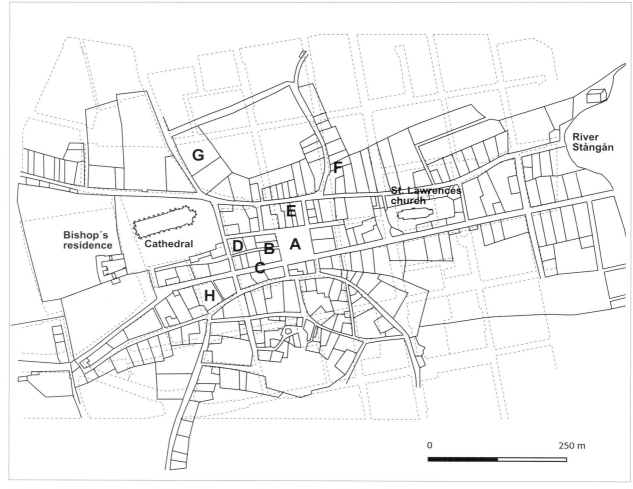

Fig. 4. The 1696 town plan and the modern town plan. A: Late medieval market place; B: The medieval High Street; C: The High Street from the seventeenth century; D: The Apoteket block; E: The Basfiolen block; F: The Brevduvan block; G: The Absalon block and the residence of All Saints; H: The Eolus block and the residence of St Andrew's. Map by the author and Lars Östlin, RAÄ.

plot (*tomt*) and a townyard (*gård*), the latter denoting a built plot with a strong identity, often associated with the person who occupied or owned it and the way it was designed.

Some examples may be given to shed light on a working method for studying the plots on the map in relation to their earlier content and development. Fig. 5 comprises parts of the main street, Storgatan, and the adjacent blocks, Apoteket and Elektriciteten. Storgatan acquired its present course in the 1650s, when it was directed right through a large block to give a straight route through the town to the new bridge over the River Stångån. In 1696 the two blocks were divided into seven plots. It could hypothetically be assumed that the plot shapes before the rerouting of Storgatan consisted of three rectangular plots between the old Storgatan and Mölnogatan.

A long section in Storgatan was documented in 1962, and an analysis of the layers shows a clear dividing line on the border between plots 23/30 and 24/29.

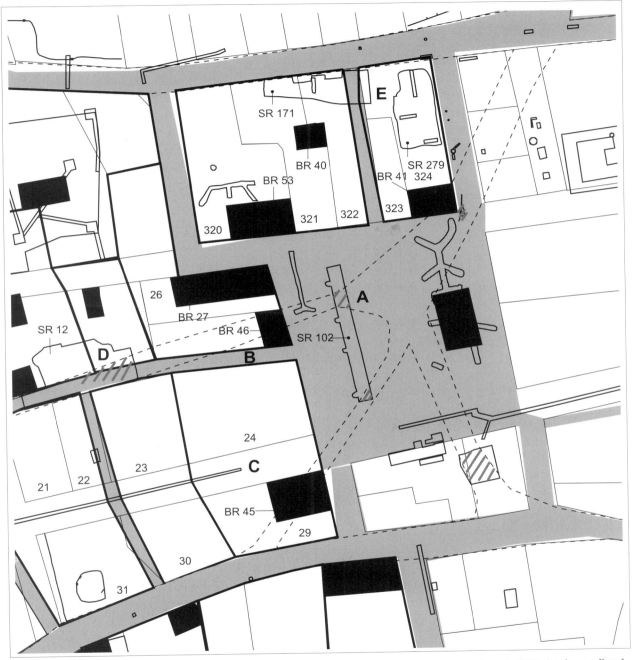

Fig. 5. The market place and adjacent blocks. A: The market place, the Town Hall and the excavations in 1980; B: The medieval High Street (Storgatan); C: The High Street (Storgatan) from the seventeenth century and the excavation in 1962; D: The high medieval street and the excavations in the Apoteket block 1970; E: The Basfiolen block and the excavations in 1979 and 1987. Medieval stone houses (black squares), high medieval streets and market place (grey), reconstructed early medieval High Street (broken line). Map by the author and Lars Östlin, RAÄ.

The difference is that a large number of layers begin and end here, a phenomenon that can be observed right from the very oldest occupation layers. This clearly shows that there was a plot boundary from the earliest days of the plots and that it constituted the boundary between two plots (fig. 5C).

The next example comes from the Basfiolen block, north of the square (fig. 5E). In 1696 the block was divided into five plots, with a tendency to boundaries running north-south, yet with strange indents in the boundaries which are difficult to explain. Two excavations in the north-eastern and northern part in 1979 and 1987 revealed settlement going back to the fourteenth century at the most. The oldest phase consisted of widely spaced buildings, replaced around 1400 by a denser structure. Both excavations uncovered simple buildings in the earliest phase, with the character of outbuildings, for example, with horizontal timbering and posts sunk in the earth. These were replaced in the fifteenth-century phase by several dwelling houses with fireplaces, built with sturdy sills sealed with clay.

Around 1400 there was simultaneously a structural change, whereby a cobbled alley divided the original plot into two. The buildings seem to have been oriented towards this alley, and the creation of two wells emphasizes the coming of a more permanent and denser occupation structure (Tagesson 1996).

A comparison with the map of 1696 shows that the course of the alley agrees well with the boundary between plots 322 and 323–324. The example can be interpreted as indicating that an older plot structure was changed around 1400, when the original large plots were divided into smaller ones. This took place at the same time as a number of other observed structural changes in the town (Feldt and Tagesson 1997, pp. 41, 152).

Fig. 5 marks three stone houses north of the market place. BR 41 is mentioned only in written sources. Plot 324 is called "the big stone house of Mattis the glass-pedlar" in 1696, and on a later map a stone house is marked on the street corner. BR 53 is a stone house mentioned in the seventeenth century, which partly

survives under a modern building in the present-day Ambrosia block. This was excavated in summer 2000, and at least the eastern part of the building can probably be dated to the Late Middle Ages (pers. com. A.-C. Feldt, Östergötland County Museum). The third stone house BR 40 is mentioned as newly constructed in the 17th century. It is plausible that the lay-out of the narrow plots are contemporary with the erection of this building, because of the peculiar form of plot nr 321.

A third example comes from the nearby Apoteket block, west of the square (fig. 5D, SR 12). The whole of this block was subject to clearance at the start of the 1970s, when the well-preserved architecture from the turn of the century was replaced by a single commercial complex. Only a small-scale excavation was carried out, in the western part, while occupation layers and a number of probable medieval cellars were bulldozed away without any documentation. The excavation was relatively comprehensive for its time, using methods intended to interpret the layers of settlement. Although it was the biggest excavation of the town in its time, it has not hitherto been of any significance in the discussions of medieval Linköping.

In the southern part of the site there was a neatly cobbled street which was interpreted as the old Storgatan. North of this were remains of buildings on at least three levels, the latest consisting of a number of closely placed simple buildings. Under this was a less dense structure with one large building along the street. The remains of buildings under this were difficult to interpret. A relatively large number of coins dates these three building levels to the period 1400s – 1650.

Further layers of sand and gravel were documented under these, interpreted in the report as the older course of Storgatan. Remains of postholes, a simple row of sill stones, and residue of fire and humus can be interpreted as remains of a simpler building along this older course of Storgatan. The orientation of these remains differed slightly, running ENE–WSW. Coin finds date this structure to the fourteenth century.

A twenty-year-old excavation in the great square, Stora Torget, can also be cited in this example. In a north–south trench in the west of the square, remains of the place where the old Storgatan entered the square were found (SR 102, Eriksson 1987). Until now it has been assumed that this was the same course as marked on the map of 1696, but the digitization of the trench showed that it was further north; instead it corresponds to the oldest course of the street in the 1970 excavation. By combining the results of two earlier excavations we thus obtain a picture of an older course of Storgatan, the old main road, the rerouting of which can be dated to around 1400. From this it follows that the plot structure in the northern part of the plot, above all plots 25 – 28, came about at the same time, and that this is the oldest possible dating of stone houses BR 46.

A fourth example comes from the Brevduvan block in the north-east of the town. A major excavation in 1987 – 89 revealed two townyards, one on either side of an alley, with the oldest dating in the mid-fourteenth century (fig. 4F). At the end of the fourteenth century the two properties had acquired a more permanent structure, with dwelling houses along the alley and outbuildings in the yard, a structure that remained the same until the changes in the sixteenth century. After a period of stagnation in the second half of the sixteenth century there was a readjustment of settlement a little way into the seventeenth century. The new buildings were in completely different locations, oriented to face the big street to the west, and the smaller alley was closed off (Feldt and Tagesson 1997, pp. 36, 41, 53).

The changed settlement pattern that has been observed in the Brevduvan block in the seventeenth century is, unfortunately, the only example hitherto in Linköping of a change in plot structure that is documented in other towns at the same time. An inward-looking medieval structure with the dwelling houses in the yard and with unpretentious sheds or booths towards the street was replaced by an outward-looking structure with the dwelling houses exposed towards the street in the early modern period (see e.g. Thomasson 1997). A comparison of the seventeenth-century buildings discovered in the Brevduvan block with the

plot map of 1696 shows that the long, narrow plots, about 10 – 12 m wide, were established at the start of the seventeenth century. Larger areas with similar narrow plots as in the example can be found in various parts of Linköping. A comparison with the written sources shows that these parts were created in the seventeenth century.

To sum up, these four examples give a picture of a retrospective method involving a combination of historical and archaeological source material and cartographical analysis. The results yield a hypothetical picture of a composite town plan, with older elements in the form of large plots, and with a documented structural change around 1400, when plots were divided and the pattern of plots and buildings changed, and another change at the start of the seventeenth century, with a new orientation of the buildings in the yards and with the establishment of a plot structure with small, narrow, uniform plots.

Stone houses

Stone houses in the form of cellars with one or more storeys built of stone and of presumed medieval date have been classified in my work as archaeological source material, with the possibility of reflecting the economic realities and social role-play of the times. They had, and to an extent still have, a physically palpable presence in the urban space and played an active part in consolidating the values and strategies of the builders and the first users. With their permanent construction technique and a completely different service life from ordinary timber houses, stone houses thus became monuments and symbols with a power that is still evident.

The stone buildings in Linköping have been listed in an archaeological register consisting of a total of 52 buildings of presumed medieval date, classified as 12 surviving buildings, 32 archaeologically known ones and 8 known from written sources. These have been analysed on the basis of material and chronology, size and plan, function, and location on the plots and in the town. The medieval stone houses have been

Fig. 6. The residence plot of Omnium Sanctorum and its main stone building. Photo: Lars Ekelund.

regarded in Swedish research as problematic because of the difficulty of dating individual buildings. These difficulties should not be underestimated; the overall possibility of dating stone houses is dealt with elsewhere (Tagesson 2002 pp. 352 ff.). In this context, only one example will be given, the still surviving stone house in the Absalon block.

The two-storey stone building is known as Rhyzelius-gården or the stone museum, while "the monastery" is a colloquial name reflecting an older idea that there was an "abbot's residence" in the medieval Franciscan friary. The long-debated location of the friary, however, was in a completely different part of the town (Tagesson 2000). After the clearance of modern buildings from the plot, the stone house was isolated in the twentieth century. Despite the prominent features of the stone house, it is still a fairly anonymous building in today's city centre (fig. 6).

The building consists of a cellar in the southern part and two storeys plus an attic. Masonry joins on the east and west sides show that the building in its oldest phase consisted of the cellar and one or possibly two storeys, with one room on each floor. The entrance to the cellar was originally in the northern part, through a door leading to a downward slope, possibly fitted with wooden steps. The entrance to the ground floor was just beside this, in the same façade.

In a second phase the house was extended towards the north and thus changed its longitudinal orientation from east-west to north-south. The building was given two rooms on the ground floor, a small one and a big one. The way down to the cellar was now inside the building, and the former door became a passage between the two rooms. The upper storey today is divided by a secondary wooden wall, but the absence of rebates or marks left by any older wall makes it uncertain whether the upper storey had more than one room. In the west façade of the upper storey there is an opening to a privy, and chopped off bricks on the west façade show that there was originally a projecting oriel on the west side.

The building material is exclusively natural stone, but with window and door surrounds of brick in Flemish double-stretcher bond. When it was rebuilt, the house was given stepped gables of brick and blind windows in the form of a cross and other shapes. The windows and doors have segmental arches.

There are no solid grounds for dating the oldest phase. The building material in the form of natural stone with brick details and segmental arches is a common feature of the majority of the known secular buildings in Linköping. About twenty of these have been dated to the Late Middle Ages, mainly through archaeological investigations, and a dating to the end of the fourteenth century or the start of the fifteenth seems reasonable for the stone house in the Absalon block. Most of the secular stone buildings in the town appear to have been built at the same time, namely, from the second half of the fourteenth century to the end of the Middle Ages.

For the dating of the addition, however, there are a few other clues. Stepped gables with blind windows have been observed on a couple of other buildings, including the bishop's palace (Linköping Castle) where they have been dated to the end of the fourteenth century and the fifteenth century (Modén in press). The three

preserved window shutters on the south façade of the stone house have also attracted attention recently. They are of a very characteristic type consisting of a frame completely filled with horizontal iron mountings and decorated with two vertical rows of small discs with punched decoration. There are two very similar doors to the sacristies in the cathedral, and a number of comparable church doors are known from Östergötland and Småland. The art historian Lennart Karlsson considers that these doors belong to a special workshop, "the Linköping group", and that the doors in the cathedral can be dated to the 1490s (Karlsson 1988 I, pp. 41 f., II, pp. 281 f.). The three extant doors can with great probability be associated with the rebuilding of the stone house, which would make a dating around 1500 plausible.

In connection with the Reformation, the building was for a short time the bishop's residence in the 1540s – 60s, but it later stood empty. In 1592 it was granted to the cathedral dean as a residence, and it was as dean that Andreas Rhyzelius lived here at the start of the eighteenth century. This was when the still surviving timber buildings were built on the plot, at the same time as the old stone house was repaired and turned into a storehouse. Visible traces of this rebuilding are the southern gable and the small extension containing a new stairway down to the cellar.

The stone buildings are on a plot which can be reconstructed fairly well. The boundary to the south and west agrees with the situation in 1696, while the plot continued a little north of Kungsgatan, a street laid out in the nineteenth century. There was a fairly extensive preliminary archaeological investigation of the plot at the start of the 1960s. The documentation did not reach the County Museum until the end of the 1980s, when a report was compiled (Tagesson 1989).

In connection with this investigation the stone house was the subject of some study, including a documentation of the masonry. Areas in the yard were also examined, resulting in the finding of half a cellar, and the remains of two other stone houses, were excavated in the south of the yard. The documentation material is very hard to interpret. Finds of late medieval pottery in one of the stone houses suggest a cautious dating of this building to the Late Middle Ages. Otherwise the finds indicate the period fourteenth–fifteenth century.

Later in the 1960s and 1970s there were also minor trench controls of the yard. Remains of a wooden house were found under the two buildings from the eighteenth century with a probable dating in the Middle Ages, and parts of a wooden building in the eastern part of the plot. Just east of the big stone house, remains have been found of cobbling on at least two levels. Latrine pits have been found west of the stone house, while the area between the two stone houses seems to have had yet another wooden building and a well.

Despite insufficiently documented excavations of the plot, we have an idea of how composite the pattern of buildings may have been. The first buildings were probably constructed in the fourteenth century, but in the fifteenth century the picture becomes clearer, with a big stone house withdrawn towards the middle of the yard. The orientation is clear, with an entrance in the big house facing away from the main street towards the yard, where several wooden houses are grouped around a cobbled courtyard. The privy of the big stone house is turned towards the street to the west, an area which, according to a document from 1695, then functioned as a byre. The same source shows that these were guest houses in the north part of the plot and that the eastern part of the plot served as a utility section. This plot structure may hypothetically have prevailed in the Middle Ages as well, as we can guess from the location and orientation of the stone houses.

Fig. 8 shows all the stone houses with known locations marked in relation to the 1696 map. Although the number of stone houses must be viewed as a minimum, there is a very clear concentration in an area around the cathedral and around the western part of the square. The retrospective method described above can give a hypothetical picture of the town's late medieval plots. This reveals a clear difference between the big plots with stone houses in the western part of the

town and the smaller plots without stone houses in the east of the town. There are some exceptions, however: some stone houses around St Lawrence's church and buildings belonging to the Franciscan friary in the south of the town.

The big yards in the western part of the town can be identified with the aid of written sources as prebends belonging to the members of the cathedral chapter. In Herman Schück's dissertation (1959) there is a thorough account of the history of the cathedral and chapter in Linköping, with a prominent role for the emergence and significance of the ecclesiastical institutions. The written evidence records the location of some of these prebends, while for others only an approximate location can be determined. By systematically using all the medieval and post-Reformation written sources mentioning prebends, it has been possible to establish the location of many of them, which is of course of the utmost importance for understanding how the urban space was organized.

To be able to link a historically known house to a particular plot in the town plan, the crucial phase is often the Reformation in the sixteenth century, when the prebends were dissolved and the properties were donated to those who had been loyal to king Gustav Vasa, or to the new, reduced cathedral chapter. For plot 261, the later Rhyzeliusgården, we know that it was empty in 1592, when it was given to the dean as a residence and simultaneously described as "the old bishop's residence". In 1572 the incumbent bishop was given permission to "restore the bishop's residence which Erik Falk and Master Claes have owned", that is, the bishop's two predecessors. In 1543 the newly elected bishop, Clas Canuti, had recently been given, among other things, the prebend of Omnium Sanctorum as a living and as compensation for the old bishop's palace which had been confiscated after the Reformation and become a royal castle.

In this way we can with great probability link a particular plot with stone houses to a prebend, which can in turn be followed in the documentary sources. Omnium Sanctorum (All Saints') was the seventh canonry of the cathedral, established in 1251 in connection with the coronation of King Valdemar. In the original donation the canonry was given a property in Linköping, the oldest information we have about any yard in the town. It is possible that this can be identified with the later known property of the canonry, but it was probably not until Omnium Sanctorum was attached to the *succentor*, the precentor's deputy, at the end of the fourteenth century, that the property was permanently occupied as a residence. With the approximate date previously assigned to the stone house in its oldest form, and with our picture of the oldest buildings on the site, it is possible to make a connection between the coming of a resident canon to the town and the change in the structure of the buildings on the plot.

The church and the urban space

The above has been a very schematic outline of the emergence of settlement in Linköping, which will be expanded and clarified elsewhere. The picture that emerges, however, is of a town in the shadow of the cathedral. From the 1230s – 40s onwards there was a vigorous expansion of the cathedral chapter, at the same time as the reconstruction of the cathedral in Gothic style. From the late 1200s and the turn of the century we have the oldest criteria of urbanization in the form of a Franciscan friary and written details of a well-developed town in an administrative and legal sense, with records of a council, seal (fig. 1), constables, and burghers (Tagesson 1998).

With the available archaeological evidence, the oldest traces of urban settlement can be dated around 1300, first in the form of ditches and fences, later in the fourteenth century as big yards sparsely occupied with buildings. At the end of the fourteenth century there was a change towards smaller but more densely built yards, with a well-established plot structure and a changed technique of house construction.

Stone houses were built on the residence plots between the cathedral and the square, often with cellars and several storeys. This late medieval structure remained until the mid-sixteenth century, although with changes to the stock of houses and with additions and modifications to the stone houses, all the time within the same structure. The sixteenth century saw a decline, probably because the Reformation had changed the church's economy. At the same time there were two devastating fires and the ravages of war in the mid-sixteenth century. When a new expansion came at the start of the seventeenth century, the older inward-looking townyard structure was replaced by a Renaissance-inspired structure in which the dwelling house faced the street. At the same time, new plots were established in new areas, long and narrow and more uniform.

If we try to tie these findings, which are in line with traditional research in urban archaeology, with the idea of using space as an analytical instrument, many new questions are raised about the picture of development outlined here. Why these spatial structures? Why sparsely built plots in the High Middle Ages? Why no stone houses before the start of the fifteenth century? Why the concentration in the area around the cathedral?

The stone houses have several features in common, and it may be worth testing different explanatory models. The stone houses are distinguished by their building material, natural stone with architectural details in brick, and by having two rooms on each floor and several floors. In Erik Lundberg's large monograph on Swedish building culture, the latter two characteristics are presented as an aristocratic feature. Development in the Middle Ages proceeded from a few multi-functional houses in prehistoric times to many mono-functional and one-room houses. The thirteenth and fourteenth centuries, however, saw the start of a development towards two-room plans in lords' dwellings, following a continental pattern (Lundberg 1940, p. 610). The two-room plan gave an opportunity for privacy in the house, with a living room separated from the dwelling quarters, and hence an opportunity for social distance. With more than one storey, the pattern could be repeated and the functional division could be further developed (fig. 7).

Fig. 7a – c. The residence yard of St Andrew's prebend. The small plan shows the reconstruction of the main stone building withdrawn from the main streets and facing a little lane. A vaulted entrance in the stone building permitted access to the yard, indicating that a fence closed the residence yard. Photos by Lars Ekelund and map by the author and Lars Östlin, RAÄ.

The phenomenon of two-room, multi-storey stone buildings in Linköping can thus be interpreted as an aristocratic feature. Details in the buildings, such as the choice of material, stepped gables, vaults, blind windows, etc. may have been modelled on the bishop's palace or other aristocratic settings. It is not entirely easy, however, to clarify the function of the buildings. The need for secure storage is emphasized by the fact that most stone houses have a cellar. Other rooms can be interpreted as private living quarters or halls, or a combination of these. It is not easy to argue for the dwelling function, however, since traces of fireplaces are missing in most of the surviving buildings, for example, the stone house in the Absalon block.

A new building at the bishop's palace, erected in the time of Bishop Henrik Tidemansson, 1465 – 1500, is described in detail in the time of his successor, Hans Brask. On the ground floor there was a kitchen and baking room, on the first floor was the bishop's chamber with a fireplace, and the top floor had a dining room

(Cnattingius 1935 – 36, p. 37). The description gives a good picture of the composite function of a multi-storey building with a two-room plan, where the storage, hall and dwelling function could be combined.

The description above may possibly give a relevant stylistic and functional explanation for the building of the stone houses, but it does not answer the question why this development occurred at the end of the fourteenth century and the start of the fifteenth. If we accept the identification of the properties with stone houses as residences, however, there is an abundance of material to drawn on in Schück's dissertation. Here one of several conceivable explanations can be sought in the church's institutional change in the Late Middle Ages, with a concentration in the diocesan capital as a consequence. Tithes were now more often paid in cash or in kind as products which were easy to sell, for example, butter. The bishop's estates which had previously been a dense network of points of economic support were replaced by tenant farms, and the col-

lected resources were concentrated in a few increasingly important residences. The port of Söderköping on the Baltic was the most important place for the sale of the church's surplus, but St Peter's market, which was held on 29 June each year in Linköping, at the same time as the annual meeting of the clergy, was probably of some significance as well. The concentration of the economic base of the chapter's prebends and the economy of the bishop's table probably led to an increase in the importance of the urban functions of the cathedral city (Schück 1959, pp. 390 ff., 466).

This explanatory model has the advantage of indicating a possible concentration of the church's economic capital in the diocesan capital in the Late Middle Ages. This generated possibilities for investment, but it does not explain why these investments took the special form they did. Parallel to the economic concentration in the town there was a development towards the increased presence of the members of the cathedral chapter, the lower canons and the higher prelates, in

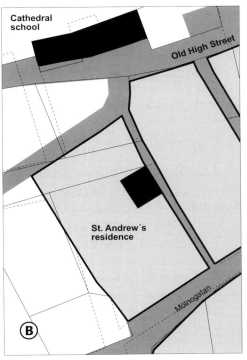

Fig. 8. The institutional town of medieval Linköping. A reconstruction of institutions, residence yards and stone buildings, with the map from 1696 in the background. 1: The residence of Omnium Sanctorum; 2: The residence of St Andrew's; 3: Bishop's palace; 4: Cathedral; 5: St Lawrence's church; 6: Town Hall; 7 Franciscan friary. Map by the author and Lars Östlin, RAÄ.

the diocesan capital (Schück 1959, pp. 437 ff.). This was a deliberate endeavour on the part of the chapter in the Late Middle Ages to increase the chapter's significance and scope for action.

The establishment of the chapter in the thirteenth century was in itself an expression of the church's aspiration for independence from the secular power. In the fifteenth century there was a further stress on the political power of the church through powerful aristocratic bishops and through the church's demand to have

sovereignty over its own resources, independent of the state. There was a tendency during the Union of Kalmar (i.e. from the end of the fourteenth century to the Reformation) for the church to struggle to retain its old privileges (Pernler 1999, pp. 107 ff.). The period after 1350 had involved great strains for the diocese of Linköping, with political unrest, reduced income, and plundered farms. When viewed in this light, we can better understand the aspiration for a resident chapter, with prebendaries on the spot in the diocesan capital.

If we study the change in spatial structure in the Late Middle Ages, a natural interpretation would be that the church was strong and self-aware. A social topography becomes visible through the use of new elements such as stone buildings with two-room plans, and several storeys, features which radically differ from secular timber architecture. Alternatively, the presence of a greater number of chapter members in the urban space and the massive expansion of properties with physically palpable stone houses could be interpreted as a deliberate and symbolically charged manifestation, in a situation when the church's old privileges had begun to be questioned.

From the end of the fourteenth century there is a development towards a conscious endeavour to highlight and accentuate an image of a concerted and powerful ecclesiastical organization. Linköping's skyline in 1500 must have been a remarkable sight. If one approached the town from the east and from the important passage over the river via the Stångebro bridge, the important main road continued towards the town. It lay there on the eastern slope of a distinct moraine ridge, with the cathedral and the bishop's palace in the foreground on the crest of the ridge. Around the cathedral the residences lay grouped, these large, sparsely built townyards, with a stone house of several storeys withdrawn from the street. Through this design they gave the impression of being dominant and inaccessible at the same time (fig. 8).

Below these properties, where the slope levelled out to a plateau, lay the square, surrounded by prebends to the east, north, and partly also on south side. In this area the townyards had stone houses in a more advanced position on the plot, which probably contrasted with the shops surrounding the square. Burgher buildings, not many of which have been investigated, were probably concentrated in the area between the square and St Lawrence's church in the east, that is, on the plateau of the square on the slope to the east. The contrast between the big prebends with stone houses and the presumably smaller burgher townyards with wooden buildings was further heightened by the po-sition on the steep slope. Moreover, the burgher houses were framed by the churchyard of St Lawrence's to the west and the large area occupied by the Franciscan friary in the south.

The main road from Stångebro led to the open square, where several highways, the framework of the town's street grid, converged. Two important streets, probably originally highways, continued up the slope, one on either side of the walled cathedral churchyard: the old Storgatan to the south and Ågatan to the north. Two more parallel streets in the south of the town, Mölnogatan-Sandgatan and the later-named Hospitalsgatan, were older communication routes linked to Storgatan. The residences were oriented to the upper part of these streets, thus framing them.

The townyards around the cathedral, large in area but not densely built, with their tower-like stone houses and massive stone architecture, contrasted with the otherwise low buildings of the town. The placing of the residences on the upper part of the eastern slope below the cathedral is a highly deliberate use of space to manifest the church's universal claims at a time when the church was suffering a crisis of legitimacy and identity. This is scarcely just a stylistic feature or a passive reflection of the social relations in late medieval society. We should rather interpret these powerful spatial expressions as active and clearly readable symbols of how the church perceived its role in the Late Middle Ages and how it wanted to be perceived. The spatial structure in the diocesan capital was thus part of a cultural system, a kind of medieval zenith, but at the same time an augury of the radically changed conditions that the Renaissance and the Reformation were to bring.

■ Göran Tagesson

Note
This article has previously appeared in Swedish in *Bebyggelsehistorisk tidskrift* 41/2001, under the title "Kyrkan och det urbana rummet".

Fig. 9. A lid from a *chrismatorium* (a tripartite vessel containing sacred oil), found by an archaeological excavation in the residence plot of Omnium Sanctorum. Photo: Göran Billeson.

References

Andersson, H. 1979. *Urbaniseringsprocessen i det medeltida Sverige. Medeltidsstaden 7.* Riksantikvarieämbetet.

Andersson, H. 1990. *Sjuttiosex medeltidsstäder – aspekter på stadsarkeologi och medeltida urbaniseringsprocess i Sverige och Finland. Medeltidsstaden 73.* Riksantikvarieämbetet.

Bartlett, A. 1994. Spatial Order and Psychiatric Disorder. In Parker Pearson, M., and Richards, C. (eds.), *Architecture and Order. Approaches to Social Space.* London and New York.

Cnattingius, B. 1935 – 36. Linköpings slott. *Meddelanden från Östergötlands Fornminnes- och museiförening 1935 – 36.*

Eriksson, J. 1987. Stora Torget – Linköpings historiska kärna. *Linköping 700 år. Meddelanden från Östergötlands Länsmuseum.*

Feldt, A.-C., and Tagesson, G. 1997. *Två gårdar i biskopens stad – om de arkeologiska undersökningarna i kvarteret Brevduvan, Linköping 1987 – 89.* Linköping.

Foucault, M. 1998. *Övervakning och straff. Fängelsets födelse.* 2nd ed. Translated by C. G. Bjurström. Lund.

Giddens, A. 1984. *The Constitution of Society. Outline of the Theory of Structuration.* Cambridge.

Gilchrist, R. 1994. *Gender and Material Culture. The Archaeology of Religious Women.* London.

Grenville, J. 1997. *Medieval Housing.* London.

Grenville, J. 2000. The Urban Household Project at York and its Archaeological Implications. In Eriksdotter, G., Larsson, S., Löndahl, V. (eds.), *Att tolka stratigrafi. Det tredje nordiska stratigrafimötet. Åland 1999.* Meddelanden från Ålands högskola 11. Åbo.

Gurevich, A. 1985. *Categories of Medieval Culture.* London.

Harrison, D. 1996. *Medieval Space. The Extent of Microspatial Knowledge in Western Europe during the Middle Ages.* Lund Studies in International History 34. Lund.

Hillier, B., and Hanson, J. 1984. *The Social Logic of Space.* Cambridge.

Karlsson, L. 1988. *Medieval Ironwork in Sweden.* I. Stockholm.

Kealhofer, L. 1999. Creating Social Identity in the Landscape: Tidewater, Virginia, 1600 – 1750. In Knapp, A. B., and Ashmore, W. (eds.), *Archaeologies of Landscape. Contemporary Perspectives.* Malden, Mass.

Knapp, A. B., and Ashmore, W. (eds.) 1999. *Archaeologies of Landscape. Contemporary Perspectives.* Malden, Mass.

Kraft, S. 1975. *Linköpings stads historia 1. Från äldsta tid till 1567.* 2nd ed. (1st ed. 1946). Linköping.

Kugelberg, A. 1972 – 75. *Gamla Linköpingsgårdar* 1 – 4. Skriftserie utgiven av föreningen Gamla Linköping (1st ed. 1943 and 1949).

Lilley, K. 2000. Mapping the Medieval City: Plan Analysis and Urban History. *Urban History* 27. Cambridge.

Lundberg, E. 1940. *Byggnadskonsten i Sverige 1000 – 1400*. Stockholm.

Modén, E. in press. Linköpings slott 900 år. *Östergötland. Meddelanden från Östergötlands Länsmuseum.*

Parker Pearson, M., and Richards, C. 1994. *Architecture and Order. Approaches to Social Space.* London and New York.

Pernler, S.-E. 1999. *Sveriges kyrkohistoria. 2. Hög- och senmedeltid.* Stockholm.

Rhyzelius, A. 1968. *Om Linköping.* Skriftserie utgiven av Föreningen Gamla Linköping 10.

Schück, H. 1959. *Ecclesia Lincopensis. Studier om Linköpingskyrkan under medeltiden och Gustav Vasa.* Stockholm.

Tagesson, G. 1989 Arkeologisk undersökning 1960 – 63. Kv Aposteln 2 och Absalon 1, Linköping. Unpublished report, Östergötlands Länsmuseum, dnr 26/89.

Tagesson, G. 1996. Kvarteret Basfiolen, Linköping, Arkeologisk undersökning 1987. Unpublished report, Riksantikvarieämbetet UV Öst.

Tagesson, G. 1997. Who Wants to Live in a Bishop's Town? On Archaeology and Change in Linköping. *Lund Archaeological Review* 1997.

Tagesson, G. 2000. Var låg Linköpings franciskankonvent? *Fornvännen* 4/2000.

Tagesson, G. 2002. In press. *Biskop och stad – aspekter av urbanisering och social topografi.*

Tagesson, G., and Wigh, B. 1994. Ben och annat skräp – om osteologi och bebyggelseutveckling i det medeltida Linköping. *Meta* 1994:2.

Thomasson, J. 1997. Private Life Made Public. One Aspect of the Emergence of the Burghers in Medieval Denmark. In Andersson, H., Carelli, P., and Ersgård, L. (eds.), *Visions of the Past. Trends and Traditions in Swedish Medieval Archaeology.* Lund Studies in Medieval Archaeology 19. RAÄ, Arkeologiska undersökningar, Skrifter 24. Stockholm.

Tilley, C. 1994. *A Phenomenology of Landscape. Places, Paths and Monuments.* Oxford.

Some Comments

This book is about medieval urbanization and its various expressions in the province of Östergötland. It is based primarily on archaeological excavations and other studies conducted in recent years. These have once again raised a number of important questions concerning the character and course of urbanization. The province has examples of the entire chronological course from the Late Iron Age to the Late Middle Ages. It has been shown that the area played an important part in Swedish state formation from the start of the Middle Ages. One of the more successful royal dynasties had its base in this province. By combining their own interests with those of the church, the kings of this dynasty were to play a major role. This prominent position was above all noticeable in the twelfth and thirteenth centuries, but the area also had a significant part to play later in the Middle Ages, even though the centre of gravity in the kingdom shifted towards the Mälaren area.

If one considers the discussion that has been carried on hitherto about urbanization and its character, the towns of Östergötland have been incorporated into the general picture of urban development in Sweden. The significance of the thirteenth century has been pointed out. Söderköping, in the east of the province, has been held up as a particular example. The importance of Söderköping in the thirteenth century has been underlined by the archaeological investigations conducted there, although the town has a twelfth-century past. Yet if we perceive urbanization as a wider concept and view the medieval town as a part of this, we obtain another, more complicated picture today. This is an outlook that recurs in most of the articles in this book. It can be applied not only to Östergötland but also to other geographical areas and brought into a broader discussion of urbanization as a whole. In my brief comments I want to concentrate on these questions, although there are other threads that could be taken up.

It is important to regard urbanization not as a process that concerns only towns in a traditional sense but as a development whereby central places of varying character and orientation were established in the landscape for economic, social, or cultural reasons. This is often closely associated with some form of exercise of power in a broad sense. The base can consist of one or more functions of an economic or administrative nature. In many cases the settlement can be densely built up, but this is not always necessary. The scale ranges from single-function places to those with highly composite functions. The medieval towns distinguish themselves from other central places by virtue of the special laws and privileges granted by the king or some other secular or spiritual authority. Our studies have mostly considered towns defined according to this criterion. It is true that these represent a highly significant category within urbanization, but if we restrict ourselves to these we find it difficult to see the entire breadth of urbanization and its implications. To develop these places with a more complex structure, it was of course necessary to have an economic, social, and power-political base that is not found in every area. The need for the functions that constitute central places of different kinds nevertheless exists in areas which lack these preconditions. In these cases the solutions are different: small harbours, castles, market places, or church sites can provide these functions. Yet it can still be difficult to draw dividing lines. To take just one example, it is sometimes hard to make a distinction between what is normally called a castle, with all its parts including an outer bailey and other adjacent structures, and what is called a town, where there is often a castle and where the urban settlement sometimes has the character of an outer bailey. In genetic terms it may also be the case that the town is the final result of a development that started with the foundation of a castle.

It may seem natural to apply a chronological perspective when we look at these different central places. There have been two different lines in research. One of them has claimed an almost evolutionist development from prehistoric central places to medieval towns. The other has seen discontinuity in development, with no particularly strong ties between the former and the latter: Yet both these lines are an oversimplification. Different types of central places have existed in parallel. The same thing applies to our own times.

If we look at the Middle Ages in Scandinavia we can see a strong geographical imbalance in the spread of towns in the strict legal sense. Northern Scandinavia had no towns, but this does not mean that there were no central places of other kinds, including those with royal influence. There was not a sufficient economic or demographic base for developing towns. In the southern parts of medieval Sweden one can likewise see an imbalance in the distribution, with a stronger system of towns in the east than in the west. Towns are thus not necessary to fulfil the functions normally associated with them. The fact that they receive borough charters from the authorities gives them a special position, naturally, but these power functions can also be exercised, for example, from a castle.

To understand the driving forces behind urbanization and its expressions, it is important to study the general structure of places and not restrict ourselves to a single type. Here archaeology has an obvious special potential. The problem is to define and identify such central places in a broad sense on the basis of the physical evidence. This must be further developed. This is the context into which the examples presented

in this volume can be put. It is a matter of a number of central places, some of which are towns, others not. Yet they all have in common the fact that they stand for central functions of importance for an area of some size. Many of them are situated in areas whose centrality is undisputed relatively far back in history. The functions need not be associated with exactly the same place. In actual fact, we can see how they are localized differently but still within the same landscape space. We have reason to discuss these questions of central areas and central places and their physiographical conditions. The places differ in topographical character. What is it that that determines the topography in individual cases? Is it possible to find shared features? And why were just some of these places selected and given a borough charter? Can we detect this? These are some questions of a more general nature that are immediately raised.

The general questions that we ask may perhaps never receive wholly general answers. This can be exemplified by the evidence from Östergötland. For both Motala and Norrköping, water power obviously played a major role, probably making up the economic base for these central places. Norrköping can be perceived as a town in the Late Middle Ages, whereas Motala never had this role, according to the written sources. Is this an illusory difference due to the source material or did the places really develop differently? In both cases there is a strong prehistoric background. For a broader discussion of the history of urbanization, this divergent development is of great significance.

Skänninge is a small medieval town but it has a complex history. Both an early medieval and a high medieval layer are clearly delineated in the archaeological evidence, both finds and structures, as well as in the town plan and the town church. It is the same place, but it undergoes great changes over time. Other stakeholders probably entered the picture. I would remind readers of the discussion that has been carried on concerning the high medieval town plan and the church, which scholars have long associated with influences from northern Germany. Did Skänninge change character between the Early Middle Ages and the High Middle

Ages as different stakeholders took over? What potential do we have to discern this in the archaeological evidence?

The most recent discussion about Linköping brings us to another question. We presume that information in the written sources gives us a basis for determining the chronology of urbanization. Göran Tagesson's studies, presented in more detail in a doctoral dissertation, show that this is far from certain. His careful analysis of the evidence of excavations and buildings archaeology from Linköping shows a different picture. There was a foundation phase in the thirteenth century, it is true, but the town was not filled out until relatively late, in fact not until the Late Middle Ages. The period of comprehensive and thoroughgoing urbanization is thus shifted far forward in time for Linköping. This also has consequences for the way the town is to be perceived and how the social aspects should be understood.

As a whole, the late medieval element in the urbanization of Östergötland has become much clearer as a result of recent years' excavations. I have already mentioned Norrköping and Linköping. Vadstena is a third example, although it is different. It is one of the few examples we have in Sweden of the emergence of a town around a monastic house, in this case a Birgittine convent. The convent occupied the buildings of a royal manor going back at least to the thirteenth century, so the place may also have had some of the character of an early central place. The town, however, was certainly a new foundation. The form taken by the interaction between the town and the convent is an interesting question: was the urban development wholly or partly autonomous, or was it entirely dependent on the convent?

This book is thus about a rather diverse collection of places. It is nevertheless important to apply a general perspective and regard them as part of an urbanization process with certain common driving forces and needs. It is also important, however, to go beyond this to see distinctive features. This may seem like a truism, but a great deal of medieval research has been either the one or the other. It is important to try to formulate the general features in a broadly perceived urbanization process, but also all the variations in it. There is not just one solution to the scholarly challenge posed by urbanization in a broad sense. This book may provide material for a discussion of this kind.

■ **Hans Andersson**

Contributors

Hans Andersson, Emeritus Professor, Institute of Archaeology, Lund University, Sandgatan 1, SE-223 50 Lund, Sweden. E-mail: Hans.Andersson@ark.lu.se.

Lars Ersgård, Associate Professor, Gotland University College, SE-621 67 Visby, Sweden. E-mail: lars.ersgard@hgo.se.

Rikard Hedvall, Archaeologist, Riksantikvarieämbetet (National Heritage Board), Archaeological Excavations Department UV Öst, Roxengatan 7, SE-582 73 Linköping, Sweden. E-mail: rikard.hedvall@raa.se.

Pär Karlsson, Archaeologist, Riksantikvarieämbetet (National Heritage Board), Archaeological Excavations Department UV Öst, Roxengatan 7, SE-582 73 Linköping, Sweden. E-mail: par.karlsson@raa.se.

Karin Lindeblad, Archaeologist, Riksantikvarieämbetet (National Heritage Board), Archaeological Excavations Department UV Öst, Roxengatan 7, SE-582 73 Linköping, Sweden. E-mail: karin.lindeblad@raa.se.

Lena Lindgren-Hertz, Unit Manager, Riksantikvarieämbetet (National Heritage Board), Archaeological Excavations Department UV Bergslagen, Box 1406, Drottninggatan 18 B, SE-701 14 Örebro, Sweden. E-mail: lena.lindgren-hertz@raa.se.

Hanna Menander, Archaeologist, Riksantikvarieämbetet (National Heritage Board), Archaeological Excavations Department UV Öst, Roxengatan 7, SE-582 73 Linköping, Sweden. E-mail: hanna.menander@raa.se.

Ann-Lili Nielsen, Archaeologist, Riksantikvarieämbetet (National Heritage Board), Archaeological Excavations Department UV Öst, Roxengatan 7, SE-582 73 Linköping, Sweden. E-mail: ann-lili.nielsen@raa.se.

Göran Tagesson, Archaeologist, Riksantikvarieämbetet (National Heritage Board), Archaeological Excavations Department UV Öst, Roxengatan 7, SE-582 73 Linköping, Sweden. E-mail: goran.tagesson@raa.se.

Since the end of the 1980s, the National Heritage Board has had an office in Linköping pursuing archaeological excavations in Östergötland. There are similar offices in four other places in Sweden.

The main sphere of activity comprises preliminary archaeological studies, inquiries, and excavations occasioned by development work.

The results of the investigations are published by each office in its own series of reports. The excavation departments also have a joint series for scholarly works and popular books.

Visit our website at www.raa.se/uv, where you will find the latest news on Swedish archaeology.

Previous publications in the series

1 Forntida svedjebruk. Om möjligheterna att spåra forntidens sved-jebruk. G. Lindman. 1991.

2 Rescue and Research. Reflections of Society in Sweden 700 – 1700 A.D. Eds. L. Ersgård, M. Holmström och K. Lamm. 1992.

3 Svedjebruket i Munkeröd. Ett exempel på periodiskt svedjebruk från yngre stenålder till medeltid i södra Bohuslän. G. Lindman. 1993.

4 Arkeologi i Attundaland. G. Andersson, A. Broberg, A. Ericsson, J. Hedlund & Ö. Hermodsson. 1994.

5 Stenskepp och Storhög. Rituell tradition och social organisation speglad i skeppssättningar från bronsålder och storhögar från järnålder. T. Artelius, R. Hernek & G. Ängeby. 1994.

6 Landscape of the monuments. A study of the passage tombs in the Cúil Irra region. S. Bergh. 1995.

7 Kring Stång. En kulturgeografisk utvärdering byggd på äldre lantmäteri-akter och historiska kartöverlägg. H. Borna Ahlqvist & C. Tollin. 1994.

8 Teoretiska perspektiv på gravundersökningar i Södermanland. A. Eriksson och J. Runcis. 1994.

9 Det inneslutna rummet – om kultiska hägnader, fornborgar och befästa gårdar i Uppland från 1300 f Kr till Kristi födelse. M. Olausson. 1995.

10 Bålverket. Om samhällsförändring och motstånd med utgångspunkt från det tidigmedeltida Bulverket i Tingstäde träsk på Gotland. J. Rönnby. 1995.

11 Samhällsstruktur och förändring under bronsåldern. Rapport från ett seminarium 29-30 september 1994 på Norrköpings Stadsmuseum i samarbete med Riksantikvarieämbetet, UV Linköping. Red. M. Larsson och A. Toll. 1995.

12 Om brunnar. Arkeologiska och botaniska studier på Håbolandet. I. Ullén, H. Ranheden, T. Eriksson & R. Engelmark. 1995.

13 Hus & Gård i det förurbana samhället – rapport från ett sektorsforsk-ningsprojekt vid Riksantikvarieämbetet. Katalog. Red. O. Kyhlberg & A. Vinberg. 1996.

14 Hus & Gård. Boplatser från mesolitikum till medeltid. Artikeldel. Hus och gård i det förurbana samhället. Red. O. Kyhlberg & A.Vinberg. 1996.

15 Medeltida landsbygd. En arkeologisk utvärdering – Forskningsöversikt, problemområden, katalog. L. Ersgård & A-M. Hållans. 1996.

16 Living by the sea. Human responses to Shore Displacement in Eastern Middle Sweden during the Stone Age. A. Åkerlund. 1996.

17 Långfärd och återkomst – skeppet i bronsålderns gravar. T. Artelius. 1996.

18 Slöinge och Borg. Stormansgårdar i öst och väst. K. Lindeblad, L. Lund-qvist, A-L. Nielsen. & L. Ersgård. 1996.

19 Religion från stenålder till medeltid. Artiklar baserade på Religionsarkeo-logiska nätverksgruppens konferens på Lövstadbruk den 1-3 december 1995. Red. K. Engdahl & A. Kaliff. 1996.

20 Metodstudier & tolkningsmöjligheter. E. Hyenstrand, M. Jakobsson, A. Nilsson, H. Ranheden & J. Rönnby. 1997.

21 Det starka landskapet. En arkeologisk studie av Leksandsbygden i Dalarna från yngre järnålder till nyare tid. L. Ersgård. 1997.

22 Carpe Scaniam. Axplock ur Skånes förflutna. Red. P. Karsten. 1997.

23 Regionalt och interregionalt. Stenåldersundersökningar i Syd-och Mellan-sverige. Red. M. Larsson & E. Olsson. 1997.

24 Visions of the Past. Trends and Traditions in Swedish Medieval Archaeo-logy. Eds. H. Andersson, P. Carelli & L. Ersgård. 1997.

25 Spiralens öga. Tjugo artiklar kring aktuell bronsåldersforskning. Red. M. Olausson. 1999.

26 Senpaleolitikum i Skåne. M. Andersson & B. Knarrström. 1999.

27 Forskaren i fält. En vänbok till Kristina Lamm. Red. K. Andersson, A. Lagerlöf & A. Åkerlund. 1999.

28 Olika perspektiv på en arkeologisk undersökning i västra Östergötland. Red. A. Kaliff. 1999.

29 Odlingslandskap och uppdragsarkeologi. Artiklar från Nätverket för arkeo-logisk agrarhistoria. Red. A. Ericsson. 1999.

30 Fragment av samtal. Tvärvetenskap med arkeologi och ortnamnsforsk-ning i bohuslänska exempel. M. Lönn. 1999.

31 Människors platser. 13 arkeologiska studier från UV. Red. FoU-gruppen vid UV. 2000.

32 Porten till Skåne. Löddeköpinge under järnålder och medeltid. Red. F. Svanberg & B. Söderberg. 2000.

33 En bok om Husbyar. Red. M. Olausson. 2000.

34 Arkeologi och paleoekologi i sydvästra Småland. Tio artiklar från Ham-nedaprojektet. Red. Per Lagerås. 2000.

35 På gården. J. Streiffert. 2001.

36 Bortglömda föreställningar. T. Artelius. 2000.

37 Dansarna från Bökeberg. Om jakt, ritualer och inlandsbosättning vid jägarstenålderns slut. P. Karsten. 2001.

38 Vem behöver en by? Kyrkheddinge, struktur och strategi under tusen år. Red. K. Schmidt Sabo. 2001.

39 Stenåldersforskning i fokus. Inblickar och utblickar i sydskandinavisk stenåldersarkeologi. Red. I. Bergenstråhle & S. Hellerström. 2001.

40 Skånska regioner. Red. A. Carlie. 2002.

41 Bärnstensbarnen. Bilder, berättelser och betraktelser. J. Runcis. 2002.

42 Hällristarnas hem. Gårdsbebyggelse och struktur i Pryssgården under bronsålder. H. Borna Ahlqvist. 2002.

43 Märkvärt, medeltida. Arkeologi ur en lång skånsk historia. Red. M. Mogren. (i tryck)

44 Bronsyxan som ting och tanke i skandinavisk senneolitikum och äldre bronsålder. L. Karlenby. 2002.